SIGNS OF THE TIMES

LAKELAND

BLUNDELL HOUSE
GOODWOOD ROAD
LONDON S.E.14

First impression 1970
Second impression 1971

ISBN 0 551 00257 3

PRINTED IN GREAT BRITAIN BY
LOWE AND BRYDONE (PRINTERS) LTD., LONDON

CONTENTS

PROLOGUE

We live in the age of the *sonic boom*—one of the less desirable consequences of the modern craze for speed, in the air as well as on land or water. In addition to the anticipated results, the shaking of windows and cracking of ceilings, it seems to be producing all sorts of unexpected side-effects. One of them was the subject of a remarkable if involuntary prophecy not long ago. A light-hearted week-end article in the *Daily Mail* ended with a forecast that any day now a golfer would return to the clubhouse with the story that his ball had stopped at the edge of the hole, and that a sonic bang had pushed it in. This was in the first column of the front page. In column seven of the same page was the story of a chip shot that left the ball on the edge of the eighteenth hole on the London Scottish course at Wimbledon Common at precisely 11.58 a.m. the previous day. There was a thud in the sky from the sonic boom, and the ball duly fell in. A magazine which drew attention to these two items carried the caption: "Instant Prophecy."

The high-pressure advertizing of our day has familiarized us with instant beverages; perhaps instant prophecy has been given less publicity. But the fact is that we are living in an age when things predicted in God's word are being unmistakeably fulfilled before our eyes. This is true of many areas of life, as later pages will suggest, but a most striking instance in recent years has been the course of events in the Middle East as they concern the state of Israel. There have been startling developments, difficult to dismiss as mere coincidence. Even secular journalists are talking about the relevance of prophecy. When press and television headlines highlight Scripture, themes, we feel that the Book is coming alive for us in no uncertain manner.

It is surprising and saddening that so many professing Christians appear to be unaware that biblical predictions are being realized before our very eyes. There is a widespread ignorance of the Scriptures involved and, even more seriously, there is considerable reluctance to discern these signs of the times. Too often such events are regarded as fortuitous and accidental. We might expect unbelievers to seek rationalized explanations of this sort, but it is tragic that those who name the name of Christ should share their scepticism.

Of course, we can well understand the reason why the whole subject of Bible prophecy has fallen into disrepute: cranks and deviationists have queered the pitch. But surely the time is now ripe for a sober, scholarly reappraisal of the whole eschatological situation. Current events are compelling a realistic assessment, and Scripture itself warns us explicitly against taking up an agnostic attitude to these matters (cf. I Thess. 4:13; 2 Peter 3:5, 8). Where God has graciously revealed His designs it is our duty to be informed, and in these studies we shall be examining various aspects of such disclosures.

We shall be careful throughout not to exceed the limits imposed by the Word. That would be inexcusable. Our sole concern is that, through the Holy Spirit, we may be made wise up to what is written, but not beyond. This is not a detailed, systematic enquiry. These chapters are no more than brief essays, in which the attempt is made, in non-technical language as far as possible, to relate the signs to the times. It is hoped that they may prove to be relevant to the days through which we are living. They aim to show that the Bible is still on the beam for 1970.

Of course, the enterprise is loaded with hazards. It is not to be expected that everyone will agree with everything that is written. "No aspect of the subject of the Lord's return is more difficult to deal with than that which relates to the 'signs' which, it is predicted, will precede that event," wrote Dr Graham Scroggie. "Dogmatic fancies have done not a little to bring the truth into ill-repute and hopes falsely founded have often led to wild exaggerations of word and deed." These we shall seek to avoid. In the past there have been those who have jumped to the conclusion that theirs was the last age. Some have even been so foolish as to fix exact dates, and even in their lifetime their rashness has been exposed. Both Hippolytus and Lactantius, whose lives spanned the transition between the third and fourth centuries after Christ, calculated that the end would come about 500 A.D. Medieval literature abounds with treatises on the signs which would precede Doomsday. Martin Luther sometimes said that he might live to see the close of the age, although on other occasions he expressed the view that this might be delayed by anything from one to four hundred years. John Wesley followed Bengel in expecting the final over-throw of the Beast in 1836.

Such attempts to pin down the fulfilment of prophecy to a precise date are unwise in themselves, and in any case doomed to disappointment. We shall do well to learn from the indiscretions even of outstanding Christain leaders in the past, and refuse to fall into the same trap. Of course, if we come to the conclusion that no signs are ever given in Scripture, we shall not look for them. But if we believe that these signs are there, then we ought to know what they are and try to trace them. Unless they are clear we should refrain from speculation.

On one occasion a group of Pharisees and Sadducees waived their traditional rivalry and formed a joint deputation. They came to Jesus, so we read in Matthew's Gospel, to put Him to the test. They tried to trick Him into a false step. They requested a sign from heaven. In other words, they wanted Him to demonstrate that He was in fact the Messiah. There were indeed miracles but these did not convince them, and they no doubt put forward naturalistic explanations of what happened, as the sceptical still do today. What they demanded was a sign that was unmistakably supernatural. The miracles were "signs on earth" —Jewish tradition held that demons and false deities were capable of supplying these, but that only the true God could give "signs from heaven". The great servants of God in Old Testament times had been concerned in the latter. Moses was associated with the gift of manna (Exodus 16:11-36). Joshua halted the sun and the moon (Josh. 10:13). Elijah called down fire from heaven (1 Kings 18:38). Samuel brought thunder and rain (1 Sam. 12:17).

The Pharisees and Sadducees sought a sign: Jesus replied by talking about signs. Like most of their contemporaries in Palestine, they were weather-wise. They knew how to make their own forecast. They needed no meteorological expert to tell them whether it would be fine on the morrow. If the sky was red in the evening, they were satisfied that a fair day was in store, but if the same glow appeared in the morning, they would expect a storm. "You know how to interpret the appearance of the sky," said Jesus, "but you cannot interpret the signs of the times" (Matt. 16:3). They were looking for some outsize sign from heaven, when they were surrounded by daily evidences that God's new age had dawned in Christ. When John the Baptizer had despatched two of his men to ask whether Jesus was really the Messiah, our Lord sent them back with this message: "Go and tell John what you have seen and heard: the blind receive their sight, the lame walk, lepers are cleansed and the deaf hear, the dead are raised up, the poor have good news preached to them" (Luke 7:22). That was evidence enough.

These signs on earth would have to suffice. The hour had not yet come for a sign from heaven. That would not be until the end, as Jesus told His disciples in His Olivet discourse. "Immediately after the tribulation of those days the sun will be darkened, and the moon will not give its light, and the stars will fall from heaven, and the powers of the heavens will be shaken; then will appear the sign of the Son of man in heaven" (Matt. 24:29,30). Until that day, no sign would be given except that of the prophet Jonah—the resurrection (Matt. 16:4).

What is to be expected, then, between the resurrection and the return of our Lord is not a sign from heaven, but signs on earth. They are "signs of the times," or, rather, of the seasons (*kairoi*). These are fixed turning-points in the course of history. In secular usage, *kairos* meant a favourable juncture, when all the auspices were right—we might speak of "the psychological moment." When the term is used in the New Testament, it signifies a special season fixed by God. In every age, then, we need to discern the signs which belong to the divine timetable. Since we now live in the age of the Church, between advents, the major turning-point ahead of us is the return of Christ to inaugurate the final aeon. As we discover from the apocalyptic exposition which our Lord gave on the Mount of Olives, some of these signs related to the period prior to the fall of Jerusalem in 70 AD, more of them relate to the whole stretch of time between departure and His coming again, and all of them point forward to that crowning event.

The New Testament draws a distinction between "the last day" and "the last days." The signs with which we are concerned appear during "the last days," but presage "the last day." "The last day" is final. It is at the end. "For this is the will of my Father," declared Jesus, "that every one who sees the Son and believes in him should have eternal life; and I will raise him up at the last day" (John 6:40; cf. 11:24; 12:48). "The last days", however, represent a lengthy period, which runs from the first advent to the second. It began when Christ came in the flesh. It will continue until He returns in glory. The Spirit was to be poured out "in the last days," according to Joel, and this began at Pentecost (Acts 2:17; Joel 2:28). It is a process which will go on until the end. We learn from Hebrews 1:2 that God has spoken to us "in these last days" through His Son. So when we read in 2 Timothy 3:1 that "in the last days there will come times of stress," the reference is not to the close of the age, but to the whole period from Christ's going away until His coming again. These are the times to which the signs properly belong.

Can we interpret them correctly today? Or are we not often too blind to see what is going on around us? These are the issues we must raise. We live in a day when weather forecasts have become increasingly accurate as a result of scientific advance: are we making comparable progress in our understanding of God's signs? In the chapters that follow we shall examine some of them. The signs relating to Israel, to the world, and to the Church will be considered against the backcloth of current events.

Chapter One

JEWS

JUNE 5th, 1967 is a new date for the history books. It was then that the Arab-Israeli tension flared up into sustained warfare. But by what appears to have been nothing short of a miracle, however it is accounted for, it was all over within a week. Israel gained a literally smashing victory. President Nasser's plan to remove what he called "the cancerous growth" of Israel from the Middle Eastern scene was destined to abject failure. So far from driving the Israelis into the sea, Egypt's own forces were pulverized in the desert. Nasser has since admitted that he lost eighty per cent of his equipment, whilst more than half his men were casualties.

Nor was this all. Disregarding the United Nations cease fire order, the Israelis went on to push back the Syrian forces to within thirty miles of Damascus, and to capture from the Jordanians all their territory west of the river. The city of Jerusalem in its entirety came under independent Jewish control for the first time in two thousand six hundred years. The extent of Israel's domain was increased in one week from eight thousand to thirty-four thousand square miles.

The world has scarcely yet recovered from the shattering impact of so phenomenal a campaign. It demands an explanation, and there are many today who were previously disinclined to recognize a divine hand in history, who are prepared to do so now. They are being compelled to concede, moreover, that God has not acted in an arbitrary manner, but strictly in line with His own disclosures of His purpose in the prophetic Scriptures.

Writing in *Life* magazine shortly after the Israelis had occupied the old city of Jerusalem and gained access to the Wailing Wall, Theodore H. White reported: 'This country is still suspended between a nightmare and a dream. Legends have been born. Prophecy has come true. A flag of Zion floats over Jerusalem for the first time since the Romans levelled the Holy City nineteen hundred years ago.' When hard-bitten journalists start talking about the fulfilment of prophecy, it is time for the world to sit up and take notice. God's plan is being worked out inexorably amid all the welter of human affairs, and nothing can stop it.

As He drew towards the close of His apocalyptic discourse on Mount Olivet, our Lord told His disciples a parable. It had to do with a fig tree. Jesus instructed His men to keep their eyes on it (Luke 21:29). It had a lesson to teach them. "As soon as its branch becomes tender and puts forth its leaves, you know that summer is near" (Matt. 24:32). The fig is almost the only tree in Palestine which loses its leaves. As the summer approaches, it is conspicuous because of its leaf buds. Every eye is upon it. It is a kind of seasonal barometer. When it shows green, then the hot season is on its way. There may be some others that do the same, as Luke's version of our Lord's saying implies, but the fig tree is the most common and is traditionally regarded as the herald of summer.

This parable from nature is employed by Jesus to emphasize the place of the Jews in God's plan. Like the fig tree, they are to be watched. When the nation begins to revive, then the end cannot be far away. The identification with Israel is unam-

16

biguous. In Joel, the Lord calls Israel His fig tree (Joel 1:7). In Matthew 21:18, 19, the cursing of the same tree stands for God's rejection of Israel. But when the fig tree that was once condemned shoots forth again, then it is a sign that God is about to resume His dealings with His ancient people. When we see all these things, then we may conclude that it is near—that is, the consummation of all things. The Arabic root from which the Hebrew word for a fig is derived means "it is time" or "the time has come." It will be noticed that the Revised Standard Version, which we are using in these studies, goes even further and has "*he* is near" (Matt. 24:33). When "the Lord will build up Zion, he will appear in his glory" (Psa.102:16). If, then, we want to know how God is working out His purpose, we need to "look at the fig tree" (Luke 21:29). That is why we are starting our enquiry with the Jews.

Recent study has re-emphasized the fact that *Heilsgeschichte* (redemption history) is simply the story of God's people. The clue to the Old Testament and to the New lies here. The Bible is in fact the record of God's dealings with the elect community. There is, of course, a bifurcation as the Church comes into view under the new covenant. But this by no means implies that God has abandoned His plans for Israel. Scripture repeatedly stresses the unconditional and permanent nature of His promises.

This element of election runs throughout the biblical narrative. Israel is specifically designated as "my chosen people, the people whom I formed for myself that they might declare my praise" (Isa. 43:20, 21). "I will take you for my people," was the word of the Lord to the children of Israel through Moses (Exod. 6:7). The birth of a nation was not a matter of political evolution but of divine choice. "I . . . have separated you from the peoples, that you should be mine," God declared (Lev. 20:26). And again: "The Lord has chosen you to be a people for his own possession, out of all the peoples that are on the face of the earth" (Deut. 14:2). The perpetual nature of this election is everywhere underlined. "And thou didst establish for thyself thy people Israel to be thy people for ever; and thou, O Lord, didst become their God" (2 Sam. 7:24).

These reiterated assurances can hardly be set aside as irrelevant or contingent when the survival of the Jews is the undeniable miracle of history. Three thousand three hundred years ago, at the outset of Israel's career, Balaam envisaged "a people dwelling alone, and not reckoning itself among the nations" (Num. 23:9). That separation has been maintained from then to now. God has promised that His chosen people will never be utterly destroyed (Lev. 26:44; Deut. 4:31; Jer. 30:11). To this day that has been the case. Despite the most determined and violent attempts to exterminate the Jews, especially under the Nazi régime in Germany, they still remain as a witness to the divine faithfulness. Adolph Saphir rightly said that Pharaoh tried to drown them but they would not drown, Nebuchadnezzar to burn them but they would not burn, and Haman to hang them but they would not hang. He added that the history of Israel is the history of miracle, even as it is the miracle of history. Recent events have only served to confirm this view. We must needs ask whether God would have so preserved the Jews from racial extinction if He has no further plans in store for them. Israel is still God's people in a peculiar sense, though not, of course, in the same sense that the Christian Church is now also the people of God. If we are to mark the signs of the times, we must watch what is happening to Israel.

The biblical promises, however, relate not only to the people but also to their land. It is only theirs because it is the Lord's. The title-deeds to what we know as Palestine are clearly made over to Israel in irrefragable assurances. Jehovah calls it "My land" (2 Chron. 7:20; Jer. 2:7;16:18 Ezek. 36:5). It is "the land of the Lord" (Hosea 9:3). In the New Testament it is designated as "the land of promise" (Heb. 11:9). The land belongs to Israel only because it has been given to them by God. "When the Most High gave to the nations their inheritance, when he separated the sons of men, he fixed the bounds of the peoples according to the number of the sons of God (Heb.:Israel)" (Deut. 32:8). The donation of the land, of course, can be traced back to the covenant with Abraham (Gen. 12:1-9; cf. 13:14-17;15:18-21). The gift is permanent, which means that Israel's final occupation of her inheritance in inevitable.

In a recent and most helpful study, Dr Wilbur M. Smith quotes from the historian of Zionism, Dr Nahum Sokolow. With reference to Leviticus 26:32-45 and Genesis 13:14,15, he forcefully declared as far back as 1919: "It is impossible to understand how it can be said that this covenant will be remembered, if the Jewish people is to continue dispersed, and is to be for ever excluded from the land here spoken of." During the hearing of the British Royal Commission on Palestine in 1937, David Ben Gurion, then chairman of the executive of the Jewish Agency for Palestine, affirmed categorically: "The Bible is our mandate.

The mandate of the League is only a recognition of this right and does not establish new things."

In the light of biblical prophecy, can the rise of Zionism and the repatriation of so many thousands of Jews be brushed aside as merely a coincidence? In 1914 there were ninety thousand Jews living in Palestine. By 1935 there were three hundred thousand. In 1948 the State of Israel was established, with six hundred thousand Jews back in the land. Now there are more than three million. "He who scattered Israel will gather him," is the word of the Lord in Jeremiah 31:10. The dispersion is a matter of history. We are persuaded that the restoration will be equally so. "In that day the Lord will extend his hand yet *a second* time to recover the remnant which is left of his people ... " (Isa. 11:11). The "second time" has not happened yet, but it is happening now.

Chapter Two

CITY

THE regular Israeli toast, "Next year at Jerusalem!" has been vindicated in a most remarkable manner. The whole city is now in Jewish hands, and the pilgrims are free to visit the place of prayer at the Wailing Wall. On June 7, 1967, after only two days' fighting, the old city of Jerusalem fell to the Israelis and both the *Kotel Ma'aravi*, or western wall, and the temple area became accessible. There was an immensely moving moment when the ram's horn was blown by an army chaplain to mark the reoccupation. The temple area has been under Muslim control since the seventh century. In various periods of history the Jews have been allowed to pray at the Wall—the only surviving relic of the temple—and down the centuries they have interceded there for the restoration of the city and the rebuilding of their sanctuary. When the city was divided in 1948, access to the Wall was denied once more.

Just seven days after the capture of the old city, at the feast of *Shavuot* (Weeks), the first mass pilgrimage took place. Dr Dwight L. Baker, chairman of the Baptist Convention in Israel, made an on-the-spot report at the time. A stream of Israelis passed through the streets of King David's city under the national flag to the sacred wall. The procession, some 200,000 strong, started at 4 a.m. The nine-mile journey was made by foot along a road that had been freshly asphalted since the takeover. The pilgrimage proper began at Mount Zion and entered by the Dung Gate to the Wailing Wall. Here prayer was offered and the Psalms of Ascent were recited (Psalms 120-134).

According to eye-witness accounts, every section of the population was represented. Members of the *kibbutzim* (collective farms) and soldiers wearing prayer shawls rubbed shoulders with the orthodox religious. Many notabilities were present, including Leonard Bernstein, the orchestral conductor, and Danny Kaye the comedian. Young mothers pushed their babies in prams beside old men who had to be helped along as they fulfilled a lifelong dream of praying at the Wall before the end of their days. Only a matter of hours before the Ascent began, bulldozers had demolished the slum dwellings which reached to within a few feet of the Wall, and opened up a huge square to accommodate the many pilgrims. The crowd moved on in one direction in an orderly manner and left through the Jaffa Gate for the new city.

For the first time since the fall of Jerusalem in 70 AD, the Jewish New Year (*Rosh Hashana*) was ushered in on the eve of Tishri by services in the synagogues in the old city. Tens of thousands, according to *The Israel Digest*, attended *Rosh Hashana* celebrations at the Wailing Wall. The area in front of the Wall was the scene of continued prayers as masses of worshippers from all over Israel joined the citizens of Jerusalem. Many of those who took part had last been present in 1948 when, of course, the Wall was accessible, but not the rest of the old city. The same source of information also tells of a similar number of pilgrims at the end of *Yom Kippur*—the Day of Atonement. Amongst the songs was the *Ani Ma'amin*—"I believe in the coming of the Messiah."

Despite pressure for the city to be placed under international control, it would seem that the Jews are back there to stay. The Israeli government, it has been said, regards the reunification of Jerusalem as a non-negotiable outcome of the six-day war. "No United Nations resolution or Arab bluster is likely to shake Israel's determination to stay in the old city," declared *Time* magazine. The more perceptive commentators realize that the roots of this resolve lie deep in the scriptural prophecies. "For the Lord has chosen Zion; he has desired it for his habitation" (Psa. 132:13). The Zionist movement, whether consciously or otherwise, has contributed to the fulfilment of ancient promises. As Dr Reinhold Niebuhr recognizes, "Judaism presupposes inextricable ties with the land of Israel and the city of David, without which Judaism cannot be truly itself." Orde Wingate—who is highly esteemed in Israel—was once asked what he had read about Zionism. "There is only one important book on the subject," he replied, "the Bible, and I have read it thoroughly."

The Old Testament abounds with prophecies about Jerusalem. The Book of Isaiah begins with "the vision of Isaiah the son of Amoz, which he saw concerning Judah and Jerusalem in the days of Uzziah, Jotham, Ahaz and Hezekiah, kings of Judah" (Is. 1:1). Through four reigns the prophetic word came to Isaiah regarding Jerusalem. He saw it besieged and delivered. He saw it again besieged and this time taken. But he saw further on: he saw it rebuilt and reinhabited. And what Isaiah envisaged, other prophets appreciated too. The desolation and final reinstatement of the holy city is the subject of repeated predictions.

The subjugation of Jerusalem until the end of the

age draws near is clearly underlined. Our Lord Himself revealed that "Jerusalem will be trodden down by the Gentiles, until the times of the Gentiles are fulfilled" (Luke 21:24). In Daniel's prophecy of what will happen until the seventieth week, he announces, with reference to "the city and the sanctuary," that "to the end there shall be war; desolations are decreed" (Dan. 9:26). It is significant that this forecast occurs in a sector of Scripture which Sir Edward Denny described as "the backbone of prophecy." This protracted disturbance will continue until "the strong covenant" of v.27 is made "with many for one week." This leads some students of prophecy to expect that a treaty will be signed recognizing the state of Israel, and that this will indicate that the seventieth week has been entered and that the eschatological programme is resumed. The word in v.27, often rendered as "covenant" when God is involved, can also simply mean a league when purely human relations are implied, as here.

In Zechariah 12:2,3 Jerusalem is depicted as "a cup of reeling" and as "a heavy stone for all the peoples." "All the nations of the earth will come together against it" (v. 3), but will not prevail. This will find its final fulfilment at the end, but it has nevertheless proved in its measure to be so in recent years. The first metaphor conjures up a picture of the nations drinking an intoxicating draught, and then staggering back in confusion. "Jerusalem, in other words," commented Professor S. R. Driver, "is represented as alluring the nations to their ruin." Jerusalem will also become "a heavy (A.V. burden-some) stone." Moffatt has "an awkward boulder." It is so weighty that those who attempt to lift it only succeed in cutting and wounding themselves.

Scholars have wondered whether this may not be a metaphor derived from the experience of quarry-men engaged in building some huge edifice like one of the temples at Baalbek. All efforts on the part of other nations to fit Israel into their preconceived political structures will be doomed to failure, and only turn out to be harmful to themselves.

The restoration of Jerusalem at the end of the age is as well attested in prophecy as the long period of Gentile domination which precedes it. So much is to take place in the holy city during the last days that the return of the Jews to its total area and their control of it has always been regarded as inevitable by those who have searched the pro-phecies. It is a fascinating exercise to read, for example, some of the major treatises on this subject written in the nineteenth or even earlier centuries, and to discover how, at a time when none of these signs had begun to appear and the Jews were still in dispersion and disgrace, confident assurances were drawn from the Word of God that His ancient people would one day be back in the land and in possession of David's city.

Yet despite the many encouraging promises in the Old Testament Scriptures concerning Jerusalem, we must not overlook the fact that before the return of our Lord there is to be a final siege of the city. For the time being it will appear to succeed, but God Himself will eventually intervene to deliver His covenant children. All this will occur within the period covered by the battle of Armageddon. According to Ezekiel 38:16 this decisive conflict will be like a storm-cloud overhanging the whole land, but Jerusalem will become the focus of interest. "For I will gather all the nations against Jerusalem to battle," the Lord announces in

Zechariah 14:2, "and the city shall be taken and the houses plundered and the women ravished; half of the city shall go into exile, but the rest of the people shall not be cut off from the city."

The attack will give every indication of being pressed to a victory at the outset. The city will be captured. Dwellings will be plundered and denuded of their contents to provide for the invaders. Half the citizens will be driven to flee for their lives, but the rest will not be torn out, as Moffatt renders it. God never leaves Himself altogether without witness. Even in the midst of Armageddon, He plants a nucleus of His chosen within the holy city. It is in this extremity of extremities, when all hell is let loose on earth, and human aid is altogether in vain, that God will step in. "Then the Lord will go forth and fight against those nations as when he fights on a day of battle" (v. 3). And, as we learn from v. 4, it is at this juncture that Christ will return to the Mount of Olives with all His saints. When the King comes again, it will be to His capital. There He will set up His millennial reign. Jerusalem will become worthy of its name. It will indeed be the city of peace.

Chapter Three

TEMPLE

THE aspirations of Jews the world over are expressed in the prayer prescribed for the use of the orthodox every morning. "Save us, O God of our salvation, and gather us together and deliver us from the nations ... May it be acceptable to Thee, Eternal, our God and the God of our fathers, that the sanctuary may be rebuilt speedily in our days and our portion assigned us in Thy law. There will we serve Thee in reverence as of old in bygone days." That persistent cry to God has at length been answered by One who is faithful to His promises. The Jew is back in the land. The holy city belongs to Israel once again, and at the Wailing Wall worship can be offered before what are taken to be stones from Herod's temple in the lower courses of masonry.

To the Jew, the Wall represents the only relic of the nation's sanctuary. Tradition has it that when the temple itself was destroyed by the Romans in 70 A.D., the shekinah glory of God remained over these few stones, and that to this day the Wall is the next best thing to the original edifice. Even though evangelical Christians may find such devotion to a holy place somewhat incongruous, we cannot overlook the intensity of faith which lies behind it. When, on the third day of the June war in 1967, the Israeli troops fought their way to the Wall, General Moshe Dayan paused there to pray and give thanks. The ram's horn was blown by a chaplain. Then thousands of ordinary soldiers streamed in to take their place. Colin Simpson was on the spot to report. "Sweating, frequently wounded, they patiently waited their turn at the Wall—covering their heads with anything available, even pieces of paper. My handkerchief, and most of my notebook, went this way. They stood there often weeping with emotion, or bright-eyed and unsmiling, their faces stiff with the day's tension. It was an electric and disturbing experience. . . . " At the Wall, Dayan declared: "We have returned to our holiest of holy places, never to depart again."

Already excavations have started, to find out whether this fragment of Herod's structure—if indeed it is so—follows the line of Solomon's temple. All this inevitably raises the question as to whether the Jews will build again. Are we to see another temple in our time? Not unnaturally, rumour has been rife. It has been whispered that the Israeli government has ordered 60,000 tons of the finest stone from Bedford, Indiana, and that five hundred rail-car loads of it are being freighted, pre-cut to precise specifications. The cornerstones are said to be already in Israel, with the two free-standing pillars—like Jachin and Boaz—cast in bronze. The Limestone Institution of America, however, is unable to trace any such shipment, and Israel's ambassador to the United States has denied the story, adding that if a temple were to be built native stone would be used.

Meanwhile, despite the fact that Israel now controls the temple area within the old city of Jerusalem, orthodox Jews are not allowed to cross it. Shortly after the reoccupation, an extraordinary meeting of the Chief Rabbinate Council issued this prohibition. Religious Jews were reminded that, according to *halacha* (the religious law), they may approach the Wall only by way of the Dung Gate from the north or the Jaffa Gate from the west. They may not enter the temple mount. This ban will remain in force, so the Council decided, until the temple has been rebuilt. Incidentally, this restriction will go far to prevent clashes between Arabs and Jews in the city, since the Muslims will continue to enjoy free access to their mosque of Al-Aksa and the Dome of the Rock.

It is the conviction of the orthodox that the temple will be rebuilt at the coming of the Messiah. There were those who held to the hope that He would appear at the feast of *Shavuot* (Weeks) seven days after the city fell. Since this did not happen, it is thought that He will come on *Shavuot* seven years later and then re-erect the temple. "Thus it appears that if the temple is to be rebuilt," concludes Dr Dwight L. Baker, "the non-religious will have to do it, and they are obviously not interested."

Meanwhile, prayers will continue to be offered at the Wailing Wall, and the erosion of the stone by kissing and beating of heads against it will not be halted. No one can see the cavities made in the masonry by such pilgrims without asking whether their importunity can have been in vain. Sometimes in the cracks between the stones there can be found pieces of crumpled paper. They contain written prayers which the pious believe will be better received by the Lord if actually inserted into the temple wall. Whilst we smile at such incredulity, we are nevertheless compelled to wonder whether their cry, "How long?" is to have its answer. There are special liturgies to be recited at the Wall. Here is one of them, for Passover Eve: "O mighty God, glorious God, truthful God, perfect

God, rebuild Thy house soon, rebuild it in our time. As a praise to Thee, as a glory to Thee rebuild Thy sanctuary in our time ... rebuild soon Thy temple ... rebuild speedily Thy sanctuary."

Rabbi Moses ben Maimon (known as Maimonides), the twelfth-century Jewish philosopher and rabbinic scholar from Spain, wrote forcefully and authoritatively on this subject, and impressed on every generation of his kinsmen the obligation to rebuild the temple whenever the land and the city were recovered. This responsibility is still realized by the religious: hence the sense of messianic expectancy amongst them is high, as we have seen. It is so strong, in fact, that the distinguished historian, Israel Eldad, has gone so far as to say: "We are at the stage where David was when he liberated Jerusalem. From that time until the construction of the temple by Solomon, only one generation passed. So will it be with us."

The study of biblical prophecy leaves us in little doubt that a third temple will be built in the latter days. We call it a third temple, since the second built by Zerubbabel, was never completely destroyed, and Herod replaced the old materials only gradually over a long period of time. Towards the close of Daniel's definitive prophecy about the seventy weeks, we learn that the apostate "prince who is to come" will "cause sacrifice and offering to cease" (Dan. 9:26, 27). And again in Daniel 12:11 we are told that "from the time that the continual burnt offering is taken away, and the abomination that makes desolate is set up, there shall be a thousand two hundred and ninety days." Our Lord Himself clearly alluded to this prophecy when He uttered His Olivet discourse. "But when you see the desolating sacrilege set up where it ought not to be (let the reader understand), then let those who are in Judea flee to the mountains" (Mark 13 : 14). The Matthaean version is even more explicit. "So when you see the desolating sacrilege spoken of by the prophet Daniel, standing in the holy place . . . " (Matt. 24 : 15). Luke adds another feature: "But when you see Jerusalem surrounded by armies, then know that its desolation has come near" (Luke 21 : 20). The reference would seem to be to the prediction of Zechariah 14 : 2, where the Lord announces that He will "gather all the nations against Jerusalem to battle."

It will be realized, of course, that what the scholars call "The Little Apocalypse" (Mark 13; Matthew 24; Luke 21) is notoriously hard to interpret, and there are varieties of approach. Some of the Olivet prophecy (namely that dealing with the fall of Jerusalem in 70 AD) has already been fulfilled, and some (namely that dealing with the end of the age) has yet to be fulfilled; and it is not always apparent which is which. Hence Dr Marcellus Kik described it as "a storehouse to prophetic students, a perplexity to lay readers, and to others a labyrinth of errant eschatological notions." Nevertheless, the repeated allusions to "the end" sufficiently indicate where the oscillations of this chapter move from 70 AD to the close of the age. "The end" is mentioned in Mark 13 : 13 immediately prior to our Lord's warning about "the desolating sacrilege" in v. 14. In Matthew 24 : 14 the period is more definitely marked out: "And this gospel of the kingdom will be preached throughout the whole world, as a testimony to all nations; and then the end will come." The fulfilment of Daniel 9 : 27 is placed at this point by our Lord.

This is confirmed by 2 Thessalonians 2:3, 4—
"Let no one deceive you in any way; for that day
will not come unless the rebellion comes first,
and the man of lawlessness is revealed, the son of
perdition, who opposes and exerts himself against
every so-called god or object of worship, so that
he takes his seat in the temple of God, proclaiming
himself to be God." The lawless one will be revealed
"in his time" (v. 6), "and the Lord Jesus will slay
him with the breath of his mouth and destroy him
by his appearing and his coming" (v. 8). Clearly, all
this is to take place at the end. But the desecration
of the temple during the great tribulation presumes
that it will have been rebuilt. If this is indeed the
correct interpretation of these passages—and we
must not be dogmatic—then we may well look for
a third temple in Jerusalem. This, of course, is to
be distinguished from the millennial temple of
Ezekiel's vision in Chapters 40-48 of his prophecy.

Although this, along with other signs of the
times, encourages us to believe that "God is working
His purpose out as year succeeds to year", it would
be unfortunate if as Christians we became so pre-
occupied with what is happening in Israel (and
among the nations) that we forgot what is the
divine plan for the Church. The missionary task
becomes even more urgent. The incentive to
personal holiness is strengthened. We are "to live
sober, upright, and godly lives in this world,
awaiting our blessed hope, the appearing of the
glory of our great God and Saviour Jesus Christ"
(Titus 2:12-13).

Chapter Four

NATIONS

ONE of the most significant consequences of the Israeli victory over the Arabs in the six-day war was the complete reoccupation of Jerusalem. During the first nineteen years of restored nationhood, Israel held only part of the holy city; the temple area and the Wailing Wall lay in Jordanian territory. But now the old city itself has been regained, and for the first time since the sixth century before Christ Jerusalem is directly under independent Jewish control.

It would seem inconceivable that Israel will be persuaded to give it up again. Suggestions have been made that the city should be accorded international status under United Nations supervision. Pope Paul has pleaded that at least the holy places might be so released. Freedom of access both to the Christian sites and to the Muslim Dome of the Rock and mosque of Al-Aksa is not at the moment denied, nor according to observers on the spot is it likely to be. But that Jerusalem itself will be surrendered is improbable in the extreme.

This raises the question as to whether a prophetic turning-point may not soon be reached. In His apocalyptic discourse on the Mount of Olives as recorded by Luke, our Lord declared that Jerusalem would be "trodden down by the Gentiles, until the times of the Gentiles are fulfilled" (Luke 21:24). The implication clearly is that when the city is no longer under the heel of the Gentiles, then this period will come to an end. Within forty years the prediction of Jesus about the fall of Jerusalem was translated into actual history, for the city was destroyed by the Roman forces, under Titus, in 70 AD. From that day onwards it has continued to be trampled over by the Gentiles. "Thy holy people possessed thy sanctuary a little while; our adversaries have trodden it down" (Isa. 63:18).

But now this is no longer so, and we are justified in assuming that "the time granted to the Gentile nations," as Knox renders the phrase in Luke 21:24, is drawing to a close. Much of biblical prophecy is concerned with the nations of the earth, and the succession of empires which rise and fall during the period of their dominance. If indeed, as we have surmised, the times of the Gentiles may now be running out, then it is incumbent on Christians to acquaint themselves with what has been revealed in God's Word about the course of history.

In order to discover the pattern of events, we have to turn to chapters two and seven in the Book of Daniel. In both these passages, the sequence of world empires is set out. It is represented under the figures of the great image and the four beasts. In Daniel two the metal colossus seen by Nebuchadnezzar in his dream is interpreted by the prophet as referring to a series of kingdoms. Most conservative exegetes have followed the traditional identification, which can be traced back as far as Jerome and even Irenaeus. This would regard the fourth of these empires as indicating Rome which, as Professor Edward J. Young pointed out, is necessitated by v. 44 which distinctly states that the messianic kingdom will be inaugurated "in the days of those kings." Were the fourth empire taken to be Greece instead of Rome, as is now fashionable amongst with the critical scholars who regard Daniel as history pretending to be prophecy, not even the first advent of Christ could be claimed as falling within the period.

It is not disputed that the head of gold depicts Babylon itself, described in Jeremiah 51:7 as "a golden cup in the Lord's hand," and by the dramatist Aeschylus as "teeming with gold." The shoulder of silver may be said to symbolize the Medo-Persian empire, noted, as Herodotus tells us, for its exactions of tribute-money from vassal states, paid mainly in silver talents. The trunk of bronze is Greece under Alexander the Great, whom Josephus portrays as "another king from the west, clad in bronze"—an allusion to Greek armour. The iron legs refer, as we have already claimed, to Rome, whose distinctive weapon was the iron-headed *pilum* or javelin. Wellington was known as the Iron Duke: Rome ruled with a rod of iron, as we say, by the exercize of military force. But the idol has clay feet, or at least clay mixed with the iron. Roman government was undermined by mob rule.

This fourfold outline corresponds with that contained in the *Almagest* or Canon of Ptolemy, the Alexandrian scientist of the second century AD. And when Edward Gibbon pictured the progression of ancient kingdoms in his *History of the Decline and Fall of the Roman Empire*, he employed the same symbolism of gold, silver, bronze and iron. This is corroborated by the further disclosures of Daniel seven, where the same sequence is presented in terms of four beasts—the lion with eagle's wings for Babylon (cf. Jer. 4:6, 7), the lopsided bear with three ribs in its mouth for Medo-Persia, the four-headed winged leopard for Greece, and the monstrosity with iron teeth for Rome. The same quartette appears in the prophecy of Hosea as used by the Lord in the punishment of His people. "So I will be to them like a lion, like a leopard I will lurk beside the way. I will fall upon them like a bear robbed of her cubs, I will tear open their breast, and there I will devour them like a lion, as a wild beast would rend them" (Hos. 13:7, 8).

It is usual to regard the figures in Daniel two and seven as complementary, and such indeed they are. They represent the empires of the ancient world as seen first by one of the monarchs involved, and then by one to whom God whispers in the ear and reveals His secrets. But, as G. H. Lang insisted, it is a general feature of Daniel's visions that each repeats only as much of what has been given before as to show how it connects with the previous one, and then each adds something material to its main burden. "Repetition is very rare in Scripture," claimed Sir Robert Anderson. That being the case, we can legitimately look for an addendum in chapter seven. This we find from v. 19 onwards. At this point the prophecy advances far beyond the times of Nebuchadnezzar or the period encompassed by his dream. We are taken on to the end of history, and supplied with details concerning the antichrist and his dealings with God's people in the final age. There is thus a link with the beast rising out of the sea in Revelation 13. "And the beast that I saw was like a leopard, its feet were like a bear's, and its mouth was like a lion's mouth" (Rev. 13:2). It is noteworthy that the fourth beast now assumes composite shape and takes up into itself the characteristics of the other three. We have moved out of the realm of ancient history and the successive empires of Babylon, Medo-Persia,

Greece and Rome. We are now in the end-time, and witnessing the apotheosis of human self-assertion and lust for power. "This beast pictures the full development and outcome of the evil that lies in the human heart," explained Lang, "which has worked there since Adam fell from God, is working there still, and in this monster will attain its full stature, horror, impiety, and will reach its doom." What we have, therefore, in Daniel two and seven is "not a scheme of universal history, but an eschatological scheme with a particular starting-point," as Professor James Barr contends.

It would seem that only when "the times of the Gentiles" have run their course will these signs of the end begin to manifest themselves. Until our Lord's own prophecy in Luke 21:24 has been fulfilled, we are not to expect any such indications. That is why previous attempts to identify the anti-christ and to fix the salient dates on the eschatological calendar have been foolishly premature. Even now we shall be wise to proceed with caution. All we are permitted to conclude is that, if in fact the times of the Gentiles are now reaching their close, then the last act in the divine drama on earth is about to begin. In preparation for this we should expect to see a regrouping of the nations to conform to the alignment implied in prophecy, particularly in Daniel and Ezekiel. This may involve some sort of confederacy (composed perhaps of ten states to correspond to the ten kings of Daniel 7:24) included within the boundaries of the former Roman Empire. Arrayed against the authority of this régime would appear to be a northern alliance, as in Ezekiel 38:2-6; an eastern bloc (Rev. 16:12); and a southern power (Dan. 11:40). But the precise identification of these groups is a matter of conjecture, and undue dogmatism is to be avoided. It is events which finally vindicate prophecy, and we cannot be sure until the time of fulfilment arrives.

The culmination of these manoeuvres on the part of the nations will be the great battle of Armageddon. "All the nations of the earth will come together" against Israel (Zech. 12:3). "The kings of the whole world" will assemble for conflict on that day: their mustering place will be at Megiddo (Rev. 16:14,16). As Dr M. R. Vincent explained, this has been "a chosen place for encampment in every contest carried on in Palestine from the days of Nebuchadnezzar." Napoleon Buonoparte called it "the world's greatest natural battlefield," and a recent television commentator noted that it is excellent tank country. Here, on "the plain of Megiddo" (Zech. 12:11), the last decisive battle of history will be fought. What is happening on the international scene today in no way renders such a climax improbable. On the contrary, there is much that would appear to confirm its likelihood. This being so, we can be confident that in our day "we have the prophetic word made more sure" (2 Peter 1:19).

Meanwhile, however, it must be our task to ensure that the gospel is spread with an intensified urgency. If indeed the time is short, the call to mission is more imperative. The fulness of the Gentiles is yet to be brought in. (Rom. 11:26). The Church must ever more actively obey the great commission of our Lord to go and "make disciples of all nations" (Matt. 28:19). It would be the supreme tragedy of our generation if we failed to gather in what might be the last great harvest of souls before the end shall come.

Chapter Five

ARABS

BIBLICAL prophecy is literally in the news just now. The headlines in the press and on television are occupied with the names of peoples and places found in the Scriptures of truth. Hardly a day passes without some reference to Israel, to Egypt, or to the Arabs. Jerusalem is one of the most talked of cities in the world. When a national daily like *The Sun* explains that "the roots of the Middle East crisis are in the pages of the Holy Bible," it is time for those who have not done so before to acquaint themselves with the divine revelation as it relates to current events.

Our concern in this chapter is with the Arabs. They loom large in political discussion today. The United Nations is trying to ensure conditions acceptable to them as well as to Israel. British policy is equally anxious not to offend them unduly. President Nasser seeks to regain his position of leadership in the Arab world. The Arab League is a significant force in the Middle East at this moment. And behind this sometimes uncomfortably aligned group of peoples, there stands the ominous strength of Russia. No assessment of the present international situation can overlook the Arabs.

All this intensification of interest has arisen since the six-day war of 1967. Israel was hedged in on three sides by Arab fores and outnumbered by twenty to one. Nasser sought to avenge his military defeat of 1956 and to wipe out the infamy. Other Arab states joined him in the venture, with the Soviet Union lending its indirect support. The incredible failure of Egypt's plot against Israel seems beyond explanation in purely human terms. Even if we discount some of the stories now being told about supernatural interventions, the hard basic facts of Israel's victory defy rational analysis. A veteran of Rommel's retreat at El Alamein confessed that the spectacle of destroyed or immobilized heavy equipment beggared anything he had ever seen. As Dr Nelson Bell has written, "one cannot help thinking that in all of this God was working out His own purposes, far above and beyond the capabilities of men or nations." We are forced to ask: Did it just happen? Or is there something more than meets the eye in it all?

The Bible makes it clear that the hatred of Arab for Jew is no modern emergence. It is deep-rooted in history. It is a "perpetual enmity" (Ezek. 35:5). It is, as Matthew Henry puts it, "hereditary malice". It stems from the age of the patriarchs and the period when the foundations of Israel were being laid by God. The Arabs are the descendants of Ishmael, born to Abram by Sarah's maid, Hagar. The promise was given that he should become the progenitor of an innumerable race (Gen. 16:10). But this prophecy was added: "He shall be a wild ass of a man, his hand against every man and every man's hand against him; and he shall dwell over against all his kinsmen." (Gen. 16:12). Professor S. R. Driver explained that this latter expression really means that Ishmael would dwell "in the face of" or "in front of" all his brethren. He went on to point out that frequently in Hebrew the words signify "on the east of," and that there may be a geographical reference. August Dillman and H. D. Leupold amongst others thought, however, that hostility or defiance was intended, and cited Job. 1:11, 6:28 and 21:31. Paul's comment in Galatians 4:29 is relevant here: "But as at that time he who was born according to the flesh persecuted him who was born according to the Spirit, so it is now."

The narrative of Genesis does not proceed much further before it faces us with another primitive instance of this same racial hatred. After Jacob had outwitted Esau and deprived him of his birthright, which had been despised, Esau conceived an implacable ill-will towards his brother and determined to wreak a dreadful revenge. "Now Esau hated Jacob because of the blessing with which his father had blessed him, and Esau said to himself, 'The days of mourning for my father are approaching; then I will kill my brother Jacob'" (Gen. 27:41). To realize that this was the inception of an abiding antipathy, we have to turn on to the opening verse of Genesis thirty-six where the identification of Esau with Edom is made. Edomites and Ishmaelites together continued to harass the children of Israel and prove a thorn in their side. Even before the land of promise was reached, the Edomites refused to allow the migrants to traverse their territory, though Moses made a perfectly reasonable request. "You shall not pass through, lest I come out with the sword against you," was the hostile reply of Edom's king (Numbers 20:18).

The unkindest cut of all, however, was administered when the Edomites actually turned against the Jews at the fall of Jerusalem in 586 BC. and joined in the cry: "Rase it, rase it! Down to its foundations" (Ps. 137:7). The strongest indictment of Edom was that they "gave over the people of Israel to the power of the sword at the time of their calamity, at the time of their final punishment"

(Ezek. 35:5). The little book of Obadiah deplores the treachery of Edom and announces: "For the violence done to your brother Jacob, shame shall cover you, and you shall be cut off forever. On the day that you stood aloof, on the day that strangers carried off his wealth, and foreigners entered his gates and cast lots for Jerusalem, you were like one of them" (Obadiah 10:11). That was their ultimate enormity.

Nowhere is the antagonism of Arab against Jew more sharply indicated than in the eighty-third Psalm. It is fascinating to learn that this very passage of Scripture was commended to the Israeli forces by their chief chaplain for use as a prayer prior to the six-day war. Its appropriateness is beyond a coincidence. "O God, do not keep silence; do not hold thy peace or be still, O God! For lo, thy enemies are in tumult; those who hate thee have raised their heads. They lay crafty plans against thy people; they consult together against thy protected ones. They say, 'Come, let us wipe them out as a nation; let the name of Israel be remembered no more!' " (Ps. 83:1-4). As noted students of prophecy have pointed out, this last verse represents almost word for word what Nasser was threatening before June 1967. We must avoid any sort of exaggeration or unwarranted speculations, but the similarity is striking. Cairo radio blared forth variations on this theme for months before the conflict broke out.

The ten-nation confederacy specified in verses 6-8 of this same Psalm is of equal interest. This roll of hostile nations, as Professor W. E. Barnes described it in his *Westminster Commentary*, includes Edom, Ishmael, Moab, the Hagrites, Gebal, Ammon, Amalek, Philistia, Tyre and Assyria.

"We know of no period in the history of Israel," claimed Bishop Perowne, "when all the various tribes here enumerated were united together for the extermination of their enemy." Professor A. F. Kirkpatrick and other expositors agree. We are therefore compelled to enquire whether a prophetic element may not be incorporated into this Psalm, with a reference to the future rather than to the past.

The passage in Ezekiel's prophecy already mentioned more than once would appear to seal the doom of Edom. "Therefore, as I live, says the Lord God, I will prepare you for blood, and blood shall pursue you; because you are guilty of blood, therefore blood shall pursue you" (Ezek. 35:6). The reason for this divine chastisement is made plain: "Because you said, 'These two nations and these two countries shall be mine, and we will take possession of them,'—although the Lord was there— therefore, as I live, says the Lord God, I will deal with you according to the anger and envy which you showed because of your hatred against them; and I will make myself known among you, when I judge you" (Ezek. 35:10, 11). Of course, all this may already have had some historical fulfilment in the disappearance of Edom as a kingdom, and the enforced assimilation of its people into Judah under John Hyrcanus in the second century B.C. But one wonders whether that is the end of the matter. The erudite eighteenth-century Hebraist, Dr Robert Lowth, Bishop of London, ventilated the view that the fate of Edom as indicated above "seems by no means to come up to the terms of the prophecy (he is dealing with a parallel passage, Isaiah 34), or to justify so high-wrought and so terrible, a description. It seems therefore reasonable," he con-

43

tinued, "to suppose, with many learned expositors, that this prophecy has a further view to events still future, to some great revolutions to be effected in later times, antecedent to that more perfect state of the kingdom of God upon earth, and serving to introduce it, which the Holy Scriptures warrant us to expect."

The possibility of such an interpretation is strengthened by the precise position of the prophecy both in Isaiah and Ezekiel, falling as it does immediately prior to predictions relating to the restoration of Israel at the end. However, time alone will tell whether this is so. Meanwhile, those who would discern the signs will continue to keep their eyes on the Arabs. As Israel's Defence Minister, Moshe Dayan, is reported to have said, any new decision to bring the Arabs into conflict with the Jews would without doubt be taken by the Soviet Union. If Russia is directly involved, then we could be moving towards the fulfilment not only of Ezekiel thirty-five, but of chapters thirty-eight and thirty-nine as well.

Chapter Six

EGYPT

SOME Bible students have asserted that there is no country in the world where the prophecies of the Old Testament have received more striking fulfilment than in the land of Egypt. Although there are scattered allusions elsewhere, the three main blocks of Scripture dealing with these predictions are to be found in Isaiah nineteen and twenty, Jeremiah forty-six and Ezekiel twenty-nine to thirty-two. Much of what we read there has already happened but some has yet to take place. In certain instances, as is often the case with prophecy, there is both a more immediate and a remote fulfilment, and such elements need to be recognized as we handle these chapters.

"One of the many amazing things about Israel's religion and culture" according to Professor Stanley B. Frost, "is the way in which Egypt counted for so little in her life." Some explanation of this attitude is to be discerned in the fact that Egypt represented everything from which the Lord had delivered Israel; it also arises from the conviction that Egypt was a nation with whom God was displeased—a nation whose doom was so plainly declared in prophecy. Israel could afford to ignore Egypt, since whatever power and prosperity she might enjoy was only for a time. Soon she would be reduced to a third-rate nation.

This, of course, is what actually happened from the sixth century B.C. onwards. The splendour and might of Egypt dwindled to a shadow. "There are few stronger contrasts in any inhabited country," commented Professor Frederic Gardiner, "than between the ancient glory, dignity, power and wealth of Egypt and its later insignificance." Her former magnificence gave way to a pale mediocrity. "Go up to Gilead, and take balm, O virgin daughter of Egypt! In vain you have used many medicines; there is no healing for you. The nations have heard of your shame, and the earth is full of your cry" (Jer. 46:11, 12). Professor F. Llewellyn Griffith can write about "The Egyptian Empire: Its Splendour and Decline," and Dr H. P. Hall refers to her brilliance and decay. These are secular historians who, consciously or otherwise, corroborate the contents of biblical prophecy.

The decline of Egypt is dealt with most fully by Ezekiel. The conquest by Babylon is foretold in some detail. In the year 605 BC. Pharaoh Necho II was defeated at Carchemish, on the river Euphrates, by Nebuchadrezzar (often referred to as Nebuchadnezzar, which may have been an Aramaic form of his name). This decisive victory marked the rise of Babylon as a world power to replace Egypt. That was the end of Egyptian dominance in politics. "It shall be the most lowly of the kingdoms," the Lord God declared, "and never again exalt itself above the nations; and I will make them so small that they will never again rule over the nations" (Ezek. 29:15). Israel would no longer be tempted to seek an alliance with Egypt. It was shown up for the broken reed it really was (Ezek. 29:6; cf. Is. 36:6).

The subsequent history of Egypt was one of pathetic eclipse. In 525 BC, after the battle of Pelusium, Egypt passed under Persian rule for two whole centuries, until Alexander the Great included it in his conquests. In 30 BC Egypt became a Roman province under Augustus. By the third century AD there was a considerable Christian community there. The Muslim conquest of Egypt took place in the seventh century. There was a series of Mameluke dynasties in the later Middle Ages, until in 1517 Egypt fell to the Ottomans, or Turks. It was not until 1922 that independence was eventually achieved and a new era in Egyptian history inaugurated. The period of decline predicted in Scripture was a lengthy one indeed. "This is a most astonishing accomplishment of a most singular prophecy," observed the eighteenth-century evangelical commentator, Thomas Scott: "for who could have conceived that so renowned and powerful a country should have been thus permanently subjected to foreigners?"

According to Ezekiel 30:13, "there shall no longer be a prince in the land of Egypt." Psammetichus III was captured by Cambyses in the year 525 BC and, from that time to this, there has never been an autonomous native-born royal ruler in Egypt. In the Babylonian and Persian eras a series of Pharaohs continued to occupy the throne, but their monarchy was only held under the surveillance of the superior power. One of these puppets was Hophra, who foolishly boasted that "not even a god could deprive him of his kingdom." It is thought that it is he who is addressed in Ezekiel 29:2-5. In 350 BC Ochus subdued the last of the rebellions, and from then on there was no further attempt to restore the line of Pharoahs. Cleopatra was a queen in the Ptolemaic dynasty, which was of Macedonian Greek origin.

Scripture, however, has more to say about Egypt than this. It not only foretells its decline:

it also prophesies a brighter future before the end. This is painted for us in the second part of Isaiah nineteen. Verses 1-15 have to do with Egypt's judgement. Verses 16-25 have to do with Egypt's hope. Part one has already been fulfilled in the course of history, as we have seen. Part two will be finally fulfilled at the close of history. The key to this second section is to be found in the recurring phrase "in that day." Not only here in Isaiah, but throughout Scripture, this is a formula referring to the end. "In that day" is not any day: it is the day of God when He will wind up His affairs on earth. It is the day of His kingdom. The expression appears five times in this passage, introducing five brief oracles concerning the end time. From verse 15 to verse 16 we pass at a bound to the Messianic period. As Professor Edmond Power points out, this latter half of the chapter has to do with "the gradual conversion of the Egyptians in Messianic times."

Yet already there had been hints in history that such things were to happen at the end. Like many another prophecy, this had an immediate and a remote fulfilment. These verses found their first vindication in events which occurred between the century of Isaiah and the first coming of Messiah, but their ultimate realisation is reserved for the time of His return. To ignore the short term reference is to weaken the historical evidence for the reliability of Scripture: to miss the ulterior significance is to deprive the passage of relevance for the present age as providing signs of the times.

In the opening verse of the second section we are told about Egypt's fear. "In that day the Egyptians will be like women, and tremble with fear before the hand which the Lord of hosts shakes over them" (Is. 19:16). This might well be a description of Egypt's reaction to Israel today. But although there are parallels now, and have been in the past, this prophecy will find its ultimate fulfilment only at the end. Yet we may legitimately wonder whether Egypt's present fear of Israel may not be an indication that the times of the Gentiles will soon have run out, and that the consummation of the kingdom may not be long delayed. The swiftness with which the Israelis dealt their knock-out blows, first in the air and then on the ground, in the Sinai desert, must have made the Egyptians realize that they were facing no ordinary enemy. Must they not ask, and must we not ask, whether the only adequate explanation lies in the purpose of the Lord of Hosts mentioned here in Isaiah 19:17?

The crux of this oracle is in v. 21: "And the Lord will make himself known to the Egyptians; and the Egyptians will know the Lord in that day" (cf. v. 18). Isaiah is the great universal prophet. He saw that God was not the God of the Jews only, but the God of the whole earth. One day He will be recognized as such. Yet Egypt has a specific place in this plan. "When they cry to the Lord . . . he will send them a saviour" (v. 20). That is the gospel of promise to Egypt, as to every people under the sun. The hope of Egypt, as of every other land, lies in our Lord and Saviour Jesus Christ. Already there are many, even in that Muslim country, who name the name of Jesus. God has not left Himself without witness there. The Coptic Church is one of the most ancient in Christendom. It numbers well over a million members, and there are nearly as many more Christians who belong to other bodies. But before the end, after the Jews have hailed their Messiah, far greater numbers in Egypt are evidently expected to bow before our God and His Christ. It may be that just as the children of Israel will one day acknowledge Jesus as Messiah, so the followers of Mahomet will acknowledge Jesus, whom they already revere as a prophet, as the Son of God. Who knows? We cannot tell. But this is sure—Egypt is to know the Lord.

The closing verses of this chapter speak about Egypt's liberty and blessing. (vv. 23-25). Egypt now, of course, is a nation in bondage. She is at the mercy of power politics. She is locked in the grip of racial conflict. The entire policy of the Middle East is determined by the antipathy of Arab and Jew. With the establishment of the State of Israel in 1948 a middle wall of partition has been erected in Palestine. There is no free passage from north to south or from east to west. All sorts of restrictions impede the normal processes of trade and travel in the Middle East. But one day there will be a highway from Egypt to Assyria. There will be freedom of movement once again. A tripartite alliance is envisaged between Israel, Egypt and Syria. Each of them, and all of them together, are to be "a blessing in the midst of the earth" (v. 24). That means not just in the middle of the world, as the geographical location suggests, but streaming out to the entire earth in all directions. From this triple alliance, untold benefits will accrue to the whole world. In a measure this was hinted at in the Persian régime. "This in turn," explains Professor Gleason Archer, "is but a foregleam of a final and more lasting peace that will be established between east and west in the days of the Messiah". Despite her past decline and present distresses, Egypt's future is bright with gospel light.

Chapter Seven

WAR

WE usually think of a telephone call as something strictly private: we do not anticipate an audience. We object to eavesdroppers on a party line. We query the right of the State to tap the wires. Our conversation is between ourselves and the person we have rung up, and we prefer it that way. Yet millions not only heard but saw a telephone conversation on Monday, July 21st, 1969—it was the most public telephone call ever! President Richard Nixon talked to the American astronauts on the moon from the Oval Room at the White House in Washington. He himself realized what a historic occasion it was. "Because of what you have done," he told Armstrong and Alldrin, "the heavens have become part of man's world." Then he added, significantly: "And as you talk to us from the Sea of Tranquillity, it inspires us to double our efforts to bring peace and tranquillity to earth."

Even on such a day of human triumph, none could forget that the world is weighed down by the fear of war. Since the dropping of the first atomic bomb, a mushroom shaped cloud has hung over all the earth like another sword of Damocles. The threat of nuclear aggression is ever present, and around the globe men keep watch day and night. And whilst we wonder if a third world war may plunge us into unimaginable horrors, the news headlines continue to remind us of conflict in Vietnam and Nigeria, and of the tense situation in the

Middle East. "Wars and rumours of wars" are the order of the day.

This, of course, is just what Jesus told us. We can expect no less. This is one of the signs of the times. We should understand that, whilst there may be an intensification before the end, war as such is not simply an eschatological factor. The times of which it is a sign are those which run from our Lord's first advent to His second. In the past, some have been misled into supposing that the return of Christ was near because of some particularly fierce contest on the field of battle, but that is to misinterpret the nature of the sign. "Wars and rumours of wars" will persist until the end. They are not themselves an indication that the day of God is approaching. They are rather a confirmation of our Lord's prediction that throughout the entire period from the ascension to the return such things will happen.

It was in the Olivet discourse that Jesus spoke about these things. The fullest version is in Matthew twenty-four which should, however, be compared with Mark thirteen and Luke twenty-one. This apocalyptic passage is one of those scriptures which it is hard to understand (Heb. 5:11, 2 Peter 3:16). In the nature of the case, unfulfilled prophecy can never be completely established before the event; but here the issue is further complicated by the fact that as we saw some of the prophecies (concerning the fall of Jerusalem) have already been fulfilled, and others (concerning the end of the age) still await fulfilment, and it is not always obvious which is which. Moreover, as we have just noted, some are in the course of being fulfilled in history.

This complex reference is reflected in the question put by the disciples to our Lord after He had foretold the destruction of the temple. "Tell us, when will this be, and what will be the sign of your coming and of the close of the age?" (Matt. 24:3). "When will this be?"—that is, the fall of Jerusalem. "What will be the sign of your coming and of the close of the age?"—that is, the return of Christ and the consummation of all things. The coming of Christ is bound up with the close of the age, and the fall of Jerusalem is a foreshadowing of it all in a way which makes it hard to sort out the allusions here in Matthew twenty-four. There are those who would confine everything to the generation before the fall of Jerusalem in 70 AD. There are those who would reserve everything for the end. Neither of these interpretations does full justice to what Jesus said. There is an oscillation between the national catastrophe and the eschatological crisis; nor is the long intermediate period overlooked.

Perhaps an analogy may help here. When an artist sets about painting a landscape, he begins by analysing his task. It will fall into three distinct parts—there is the foreground, the middle distance, and the background. He will study each of these with the utmost attention, and establish the relationship between them before he takes up his brush. Jesus has drawn a historical landscape in this remarkable conspectus, and we can distinguish the same divisions. There is the foreground—the destruction of the temple. There is the middle distance—conditions in the world during the intervening period. There is the background—the end of the age and the coming of Christ.

"You will hear of wars and rumours of wars," declares our Lord (Matt. 24:6). The New English

Bible has: "the noise of battle near at hand and the news of battles far away," which recaptures the play on words in the Greek. Luke 21:9 has "wars and tumults." This is a sign of the times which belongs not only to the beginning and the end, but throughout. Even in the short interval prior to 70 AD strife, insurrection and war filled both Palestine and other parts of the Roman Empire. Four of the emperors met a violent death within eighteen months. We learn from Philo and Josephus that this was a particularly turbulent time for the Jews. There was an uprising against them in Alexandria, which led to complaints against Flaccus and his ultimate deposition. Over fifty thousand were slain in Seleucia. Twenty thousand died in Caesarea in a battle with the Syrians. Many towns and villages became armed camps. According to Tacitus, constant rumours of war kept the Jewish people in an unsettled state. There were threats against them by Caligula, Claudius and Nero. Of the first of these, Josephus wrote that "it would have brought extermination to the Jewish nation had it not been for Caligula's death."

But when all this had occurred, the end was not yet (Matt. 24:6). The noun *telos* signifies the goal and, in an eschatological context as here, the last act of the cosmic drama. The Arndt-Gingrich lexicon places Matthew 24:6 firmly in this category. The end, then, is not the fall of Jerusalem. The end is at the close of the age. These wars and rumours of wars will continue. "Nation will rise against nation, and kingdom against kingdom" (Matt. 24:7). The first represents a body of people held together by the same customs, the second represents a body of people held together by one ruler or government. All this is but "the beginning of the sufferings" (Matt. 24:8). It is the prelude to final tribulation. War, like other signs of the times, marks the whole era until the return of Christ. The signs of the end itself are not new phenomena, but, as Dr Graham Scroggie insisted, "the accentuation and spread of evils that have always been present."

War clearly falls into that category. It is a feature of every age. On the basis of the computation in the Moscow Gazette, Gustave Valbert in his day could report that "from the year 1496 BC to 1861 AD, in 3,358 years there were 227 years of peace and 3,130 years of war, or thirteen years of war to every year of peace. Within the last three centuries there have been 286 wars in Europe." He added that "from the year 1500 BC to 1860 AD more than 8,000 treaties of peace, which were meant to remain in force for ever, were concluded. The average time they remained in force was two years."

More recently the intensity has been increased. Up to 1914 the world had never been free from war, but on the other hand war had never been universal. But from 1914 to 1918 total war was waged, and again from 1939 to 1945. In that last year, only twelve small nations were not actually or technically involved. Since then there has been conflict in Indo-China (as it then was). Korea, Congo, Cuba, Vietnam, Nigeria, the Middle East, and between India and Pakistan—to name only a selection of the military zones. Pandit Nehru told the United Nations General Assembly before his death that "World War II has never ended." It has been estimated that more than one hundred million people have been killed in wars on this planet since the nineteenth century began.

War, then, is a sign of the times. It may also be a sign of the end, but until that comes we cannot tell. It would be rash to conclude that even a third world war was to be the last. But the continued news in the press and on radio and television only serves to underscore the prophecy of our Lord. He told us no less. "This must take place" (Mat. 24:6). There is a certain grim inevitability about it. This does not mean, of course, that Christians approve of war or think that it is a good thing simply because it confirms the Scriptures. There is no such thing as a good war. Dr Samuel Johnson rightly laughed at Lord Kames's view that war had its value, since so much courage was brought out by it. "A fire might as well be considered a good thing," the Doctor replied. "There are the bravery and address of the firemen in extinguishing it; there is much humanity exerted in saving the lives and properties of the poor sufferers; yet, after all this, who can say that fire is a good thing?"

Earl Haig declared: "It is the business of the Church to make my business impossible." That must always be the endeavour of Christians. We are to be peacemakers, not warmongers. Yet although we do all we can towards this end, we are not deluded. What William James called "the war against war" will not be won until Christ returns to establish His kingdom of peace. "He shall judge between the nations, and shall decide for many peoples; and they shall beat their swords into ploughshares, and their spears into pruning-hooks; nation shall not lift up sword against nation, neither shall they learn war any more" (Isa. 2:4).

Chapter Eight

FAMINE

IT was the seventeenth-century poet, John Dryden, who described famine in a vivid phase. He called it "death in an undress of skin and bone." There was a time when only those who had travelled to the under-privileged areas of the world had any real idea of what that meant, but now television has brought the stark fact of hunger into our homes. We can see the emaciated bodies and swollen bellies of Biafran children or of Indian peasants in Bihar. And if the screen is not enough to remind us that we live in an underfed world, the Oxfam advertisements bring it home to us with the utmost effectiveness. We realize that we are part of one family and cannot remain indifferent to the suffering of others.

One of the most challenging books of recent years is Colin Morris's *Include Me Out*.* It is a passionate plea for Christians to realize their involvement in the agony of the world. It was touched off by an incident in Zambia, where the author exercized his ministry. One day he found a dead man literally on his doorstep. He was a victim of hunger. An autopsy revealed that his stomach contained nothing but a few leaves and a tiny ball of grass. That was all he could find to eat. For Colin Morris that man became a symbol of the world's need. We cannot sit back comfortably in our foam-rubber armchairs, and forget the torment of our fellows. And much of it is due to hunger.

* Epworth Press, London, 1968.

Amongst the signs of the times listed by our Lord in His apocalyptic discourse is famine. It is part of "the beginning of the sufferings" (Matt. 24:8). As it is mentioned separately, it is thought to be not simply the result of war but a scourge in itself. It is in the plural—"famines"—and these will occur, Jesus said, "in various places" (Matt. 24:7). There are other references in the New Testament. Paul includes famine as one of the calamities which may threaten us, yet will not cut us off from the love of God in Christ Jesus our Lord (Rom. 8:35), and in the visions of the Apocalypse, the black horse symbolises the same dire phenomenon (Rev. 6:5,6).

According to A. E. Taylor in a Food Research Institute enquiry, "famine is like insanity, hard to define but glaring enough when recognized. . . . One country will define as food shortage what another country would call famine." In fact, such shortages may well be relieved before they actually degenerate into famines. We may adopt the definition provided in the *International Encylopedia of the Social Sciences*: "True famine is shortage of total food so extreme and protracted as to result in widespread persisting hunger, notable emaciation in many of the affected population, and a considerable elevation of community death rate attributable at least in part to deaths from starvation." Whilst appreciating the exactitude of such a statement, we must not allow ourselves to forget that beneath this somewhat academic language there lies an excruciating human experience, to which thousands in the world today are no strangers.

The consequences of famine are distressing in the extreme. That is why television commentators warn us about them when they are coming up on the screen, in case we are too squeamish to face them. People grow painfully thin, increasingly weak, and chronically listless. In the end they can do no more than lie in their homes or out on the street, utterly inactive, barely living skeletons, waiting for death to claim and release them. No-one who has visited India, where famine is endemic, can fail to be appalled by such conditions. To step over bodies by the roadside not knowing whether they are dead or alive, is a shattering experience, but it ensures that one can never forget that ours is a hungry world in which starvation is the commonest cause of death.

Reporters tell of the incredible extremes to which the famine-stricken will go to find food and stay alive. Victor Kravchenko, in *I Chose Freedom*, describes the famine of 1932-3 in Soviet Russia. A young peasant woman told him: "We've eaten everything we could lay our hands on – cats, dogs, field-mice, birds. When it's light tomorrow you will see the trees stripped of their bark ... And the horse manure has been eaten. Sometimes there are whole grains in it." We are reminded of the famine in Samaria when Benhadad besieged it. "An ass's head was sold for eighty shekels of silver, and the fourth part of a kab of dove's dung for five shekels of silver" (2 Kings 6:25).

Famines arising from natural causes, as distinct from those induced by wartime blockades, are due to drought, excessive rains or floods, exceptionally cold weather, typhoons and other high winds, tidal waves, depredations by vermin, such insects as locusts, or plant diseases. According to the experts, their geographical incidence is purely local— bearing out the precision of our Lord's reference to "various places" (Matt. 24:7). Famine has never been world-wide or even continent-wide. Some areas seem to have escaped altogether—Australia, the East Indies and Southern Africa. Amongst the great famines of history, the following may be picked out:— India (650 AD), England (1005), Mexico (1051), Egypt (1064-1072), India (1344-1345), England (1586), Japan (1732-1733), Bengal (1769-1770—one-third of the population perished), India (1790-1792 – the Doji Bari or skull famine, so called because of the numbers who died were too great for burial), Japan (1832-1836), Ireland (1845-1849), Persia (1871), Asia Minor (1871-1874), India (1876-78), Brazil (1877), North China (1877-1878), Morocco (1876-78), Russia (1891-1892), India (1899-1901), Russia (1905), China (1916), Russia (1921), Russia (1932-1933). It will be seen that India, Russia and China have been most affected.

All this supplies a tragic corroboration of our Lord's prediction that famine is a sign of the times which run from His ascension to His return. Fulfilment began even before the fall of Jerusalem. In Acts 11:28 we read of the famine during the reign of Claudius, probably about 45 AD. Suetonius speaks of "continual droughts," and Tacitus refers to "dearth of crops and thence famine." The Christians in Jerusalem suffered greatly and Paul organized a relief fund for them. But famine has continued to mark the whole of the Christian era, as Jesus said it would. It may be even worse before the end, but its presence in the world today does not in itself constitute a hint that the close of the age is approaching. It rather suggests that we are still in the birth-pangs before the new aeon dawns.

A factor, however, has emerged in recent days

which may suggest that famine is to become an even more serious threat before long. "There is only one problem in the world today," declares Dr J. W. Evans, "and it is not the nuclear threat or warring nations. The only problem is food and population." It is in this conjunction that the peril for the future lies. The population explosion, of which we hear so much, means that numbers are outpacing the food supply. Production is unable to keep up with reproduction. Mouths are more numerous than means to fill them. It is said that world famine is now a possibility. This was forecast as far back as 1949 by William Vogt in *Road to Survival*. There is no way out. Millions are going to die. Mankind must inevitably starve "on the twin altars of uncontrolled human reproduction and uncontrolled abuse of land's resources."

At the present time, the World Health Organization estimates that between three and five hundred million are suffering from serious malnutrition and hunger. Approximately one-third of the world is well-fed, one-third is underfed, and one-third is starving. Four millions a year die of starvation and seventy per cent of children under six are undernourished. To put it more arrestingly, thirty people die of starvation every minute. The American Freedom from Hunger Foundation recently reported that hunger around the world has reached an acute stage, and that general famine looms on the horizon. Dr Ewell, Vice-President for Research in the State University of New York, believes that "the greatest disaster in the world's history is just around the corner". According to his judgment, a world famine striking hundreds of millions and even billions of human beings is near. "It seems likely that the famine will reach serious proportions in

India, Pakistan and China in the early 1970s, followed by Indonesia, Iran, Turkey, Egypt and several other countries within a few years, and then followed by most of the other countries of Asia, Africa, and Latin America in 1980. All this seems inevitable because of the rapid increase in the world's population."

For the same reason, Sir Julian Huxley has gone on record as affirming that "the human race stands at the greatest crisis of its existence and it is doubtful if it can survive." In view of these staggering prognostications, there are those who consider it legitimate to wonder whether the sign of famine is reaching its climax and pointing to the imminence of the end. Only events will determine whether this indeed is so. Meanwhile, Christians must be to the fore in bringing relief to the victims of hunger. No service can be more expressive of Christ's compassion than this. He who fed the multitude calls us to this task. "I was hungry and you gave me food, I was thirsty and you gave me drink" (Matt. 25:35). And if we ask: "Lord when did we see thee hungry and feed thee, or thirsty and give thee drink?" He will answer: "Truly, I say to you, as you did it to one of the least of these my brethren, you did it to me" (Matt. 25:37, 40). No interpretative refinement must be allowed to blunt the keen challenge of that parable. We must all ask with Suzanne de Diétrich: "How many times have we passed by Him without recognizing Him?" He comes to us under the figure of the starving, as well as of the immigrant, the refugee, the prisoner, and we turn away or treat such people with humiliating condescension. One day He will say to us: "That was I."

Chapter Nine

EARTHQUAKES

ONE of the most disastrous earthquakes ever to
hit the headlines struck the city of Lisbon on
November 1st, 1755. The shock was felt all over
Spain as well as Portugal. It came absolutely without warning. Its epicentre was beneath the sea,
some distance to the west of Lisbon. Three successive strokes of disturbance destroyed all the
houses in the lower part of the city. The sea itself
was forced back, and then rolled in at a height of
forty feet above the usual level. This enormous
ebb and flow continued all day and most of the
night. Similar waves were seen all along the
Spanish coast, at Tangier and Funchal, along the
coast of Holland, on the south and east coasts of
the British Isles, and even across the Atlantic in
Antigua, Martinique and Barbados. Yet more remarkable and exceptional was the agitation of
inland waters far beyond the limits of the area of
impact. Lakes in Switzerland and Italy were set
in oscillation. Even Loch Lomond and Loch Ness in
Scotland, over twelve hundred miles away, were
affected.

It is not surprising that such an outsize earthquake should make news all around the world. No
less than 60,000 people were killed and many
others injured. In churches everywhere prayers
were offered for those who had been bereaved, and
for the recovery of the maimed. But, more than
that, preachers were so solemnized by the
devastating occurrence that they urged their con-

gregations to see in it a sign of divine displeasure and impending judgment. John Wesley issued a pamphlet entitled *Serious Thoughts occasioned by the late Earthquake at Lisbon* in much the same vein. "Is there indeed a God that judges the world?" he asked. "And is He now making inquisition for blood? If so, it is not surprising that He should begin there, where so much blood has been poured on the ground like water! where so many brave men have been murdered, in the most base and cowardly as well as barbarous manner, almost every day, as well as every night, while none regarded or laid it to heart.... How long has their blood been crying from the earth! Yea, how long has that bloody House of Mercy (the Inquisition), the scandal not only of all religion, but even of human nature, stood to insult both heaven and earth! 'And shall I not visit for these things, saith the Lord? Shall not my soul be avenged on such a city as this?' "

Nowadays an earthquake abroad would be unlikely to produce many sermons in England. We would be less ready than Wesley to interpret such natural phenomena, however catastrophic, in terms of divine sanctions against wrongdoing. Whether he was right or we are right is a matter for discussion. But Wesley also saw in the Lisbon disaster a fulfilment of our Lord's words in Matthew 24:7 that one of the signs of the times is that there will be "earthquakes in various places." Wesley pointed out that *seismoi* there covers not only earthquakes, but concussions or shakings arising from them. He had read about the widespread effect of the Lisbon disturbance and related it to prophecy.

As in the case of war and famine, this is a sign

of the times rather than a sign of the end, although it may become the latter also. Many earthquakes occurred even before the fall of Jerusalem. There was, of course, a severe tremor in the city itself when Jesus died on the cross. The curtain of the temple was torn in two from top to bottom (Matt. 27:51). The earth shook and the rocks split. Graves were opened and the bodies of saints were raised. When the tough Roman centurion saw the earthquake and its consequences, he was compelled to confess Jesus as son of God (Matt. 27:54). In Acts 16:26 we read that there was "a great earthquake" when Paul and Silas were in prison at Philippi. It was so violent that the foundations of the jail were shaken, all the doors burst open, and the prisoners found that their fetters were unfastened.

Contemporary historians recorded earthquakes within the next few years in Crete, Chios, Samos, Campania and Judaea, and at Rome, Smyrna, Miletus, Laodicea, Hierapolis, Colosse, Pompei and Apamania in Phrygia. "How often have cities of Asia and Achaia fallen with one fatal shock!" wrote Seneca. "How many cities have been swallowed up in Syria, how many in Macedonia! How often has Cyprus been wasted by this calamity! How often has Paphos become a ruin! News has often been brought to us of the demolition of whole cities at once."

Earthquakes have continued to mark the course of history down to the present time; there has never been any let-up in their frequency. They occur mainly in volcanic and mountainous regions, especially around the Pacific coasts, the Mediterranean area, in Asia Minor, in the Himalayas and in Indonesia. The chief causes are thought to be faulting and subterranean volcanic activity. It was not until the middle of the nineteenth century that seismology emerged as a science. The term was introduced in 1858 by Robert Mallet. He produced a seismic map of the world, and also compiled a catalogue of 6,831 major shocks from the year 1606 BC to his own time.

Statistics derived from the *World Almanac*, based on a geodetic survey, reveal that there were only six earthquakes of strength six or more beween 1800 and 1896. But in each decade from 1897 until 1946 there were either two or three, and in the decade from 1947 to 1956 there were seven. From 1957 to 1966 there were no less than seventeen. This is a striking acceleration – is it significant? Does it perhaps mean that the sign of the times is developing into a sign of the end? We can but ask the question; only the future can yield the answer.

Amongst the serious earthquakes of the last decade we may include the following: *1960*— Iran: 700 dead and 7,000 homeless in the village of Lar. Chile: a whole island sunk and hundreds killed. *1961* – Japan: 10,000 dead. *1962* – Florida: 7,660 dead. *1963*—Kashmir (the worst in their history) – 58 villages destroyed. Yugoslavia: 1,029 dead at Skopje. *1964*—Alaska: with 12,000 after-shocks which released energy equivalent to a hundred underground nuclear explosions of 100 megatons each, i.e. 500,000 times the force of the nuclear bomb dropped on Hiroshima. *1965*—Red China, when a magnitude of 7.5 was recorded (Ricter scale): 30,000 injured or killed. *1966* – Turkey; the whole village of Varto wiped out with 3,000 dead. *1967*—1,000 dead in Adapazari, Western Turkey. Debar, near the Yugo-Slav-

Albanian border—7,000 homeless. Karna Nagar, India: 100 killed, 1,500 injured. 1968—Western Sicily: 10,000 homeless. Philippines: Island of Luzon. Many lives were lost in Manila.

Television has enabled us to realize the incredible devastation caused by earthquakes. Mere description cannot begin to convey the havoc. As cameras pan around the scene to show the collapse of buildings and the damage to property, something of the tragedy involved is impressed upon us. Even now in Manila the evidences are still there to be seen, where towering blocks of flats were reduced to rubble. To be involved in an earthquake must be one of the most terrifying experiences in life, as those who have lived to tell their story can testify.

For the Bible earthquakes are a recognized eschatological feature. Isaiah envisages the day of the Lord when "men shall enter the caves of the rocks and the holes of the ground, from before the terror of the Lord, and from the glory of his majesty, when he rises to terrify the earth" (Is. 2:19). In doing so, as Dr Stanley B. Frost points out, "he supplies what is to become one of the recurring features of apocalyptic imagery, the earthquake and the convulsion of nature." It is to be found again in Isaiah 13:13—"Therefore I will make the heavens tremble, and the earth will be shaken out of its place, at the wrath of the Lord of hosts in the day of his fierce anger;" and yet again in Isaiah 24:18-20: "For the windows of heaven are opened, and the foundations of the earth tremble. The earth is utterly broken, the earth is rent asunder, the earth is violently shaken. The earth staggers like a drunken man, it sways like a hut;

its transgression lies heavy upon it, and it falls, and will not rise again."

This earthquake *motif* reappears in Joel (3:16) and Haggai (2:6). It is carried over into the New Testament not only in our Lord's apocalyptic discourse, but also in the Book of the Revelation. It is noteworthy that no less than five earthquakes are mentioned (Rev. 6:12; 8:5; 11:13, 19; 16:18). Immediately after the breaking of the sixth seal to inaugurate the day of divine wrath, we read that there was "a great earthquake" (Rev. 6:12). Some prefer to take this as a symbol for the destruction of the present social order, but, as Professor John F. Walvoord argues, there are several good reasons for adopting a literal interpretation. Another earthquake is associated with the casting of fire on the earth in judgment (Rev. 8:5). After the resurrection of the two witnesses, "a great earthquake" destroys a tenth part of the city of Jerusalem and seven thousand people are killed (Rev. 11:13). When the temple of God is opened in heaven and the ark of His covenant is disclosed, there come forth flashes of lightning and peals of thunder, an earthquake and a hailstorm (Rev. 11:19); and when the seventh angel has poured his vial on the air and the loud voice from the sanctuary cries, "It is over," we read of the earthquake of all earthquakes (Rev. 16:18). There has been none like it in human history. It is so violent that the city is split into three, and the whole earth feels its effects (Rev. 16:19). It is to this earthquake at the end that all other disturbances point.

It is in this sense that earthquakes constitute a sign not only of our times, but of the last time. We do not know which will be the final tremor, but each one that precedes it warns us of it.

Geologists wonder whether the current rise in the earthquake rate may not indicate a serious condition in the crust of our planet. If this is indeed so, then conditions could be building up for the mighty shaking at the end.

Chapter Ten

DISEASE

THE experienced traveller of today always keeps his passport handy. Without it he cannot leave for any foreign land. Along with it—secured inside it, if he is wise—he will also have his vaccination certificates. These will vary in number according to the places he is likely to visit. Proof is required that he has received the injections necessary to protect him from smallpox, yellow fever, cholera, typhoid fever and the like. This service is now provided in any doctor's surgery and is a routine procedure. The doctor's signature must be authenticated by the confirmation of the local health authority. Travel agents will tell their customers what certificates they will need for the countries to which they intend to go. If these include malarial areas, they will be advised to begin a course of daraprim tablets before they leave and to take them weekly throughout their stay. Missionaries call these "Sunday pills," since they find it helpful to have their dose on that day.

Such precautions remind us that all over the world today there is a battle to be waged against disease. Before the traveller is allowed to enter a country he must not only pass through customs and immigration, but must also satisfy the health officials. In this way the spread of the great epidemic scourges is held in check. Were it not for such restraints, the plagues of the past might well take their toll again. Despite all these measures, outbreaks do still occur, although it is now possible to localize them.

Amongst the signs of the times mentioned by our Lord in His Olivet discourse there is a reference to "pestilences" (Luke 21:11; Matt. 24:7 in some MSS). They are listed after earthquakes and famines. The term recorded by Luke the physician is part of the recognised medical vocabulary. It means a plague, and is so rendered by most modern versions. According to Dr A. P. Waterson, it describes any epidemic disease and is not simply the equivalent of the modern infection with *Pasteurella pestis*. This is the only instance in the New Testament where the word *loimos* is used to denote actual plagues. In Acts 24:5 it is applied by Tertullus to the apostle Paul. "For we have found this man a pestilent fellow, an agitator among all the Jews throughout the world, and a ringleader of the sect of the Nazarenes." Literally the Greek here is "a pestilence," and the New English Bible hits it off admirably when it makes Tertullus report: "We have found this man to be a perfect pest."

It is a grim reminder of how lethal the plague invariably turned out to be that in the Septuagint (the Greek Old Testament), the Hebrew word *deber* is frequently translated simply as "death." That was what pestilence spelt in ancient times, and still does today where it is not curbed. When Jesus prophesied that, throughout the period from His departure until His return, disease would stalk the face of the earth, He was stating what history has shown to be a plain and uncomfortable fact. With all our modern prophylactics, there are many parts of the world in which the battle for health has not yet been won.

It is not accidental that our Lord speaks of famine and pestilence in the same breath. These twin terrors are interrelated: the one breeds the other. Lack of food reduces resistance and makes men prone to disease. In the Old Testament—especially in Jeremiah's prophecy—famine and pestilence are linked with the sword. 2 Chronicles 20:9 includes judgment along with them—unless the reference is to "the sword of judgment," as the RSV footnote suggests. The inclusion of judgment interprets the rest. War, famine, pestilence as signs of the times are also perpetual reminders of the divine displeasure with man's sin. Secular man wants to settle down in his materialistic world, and delude himself that he has no need of any external reference. God will never allow him to do so. Again and again these disturbances intrude to shake man out of his complacency and compel him to think again.

Even before the fall of Jerusalem the Olivet prediction of our Lord found a sufficiently solemnizing fulfilment. In the year 65 AD a plague in Rome itself carried off 30,000 people in a single autumn. Suetonius alludes to it and says that the names were registered in the temple of Libitina. From that time onwards the chronicles of history record a dreadful sequence. The physician Rufus of Ephesus, who lived in the time of the emperor Trajan, speaks of "the buboes called pestilential" as being specially fatal and found chiefly in Libya, Egypt and Syria. In the sixth century the bubonic plague spread to Europe as part of a recurring cycle which affected the whole Roman world for fifty years. The following century teems with pestilences—the Venerable Bede in his account of the Church in England mentions four distinct waves between 664 and 683.

Procopius has left an accurate and convincing record of such an outbreak in Constantinople when Justinian was emperor. He describes the disease as arising in Egypt and thence extending its tentacles in every direction. In the city, he tells us, "it lasted four months. At the beginning only a few more persons died than ordinarily, but afterwards as the evil increased the number of the dead reached five thousand a day, and subsequently ten thousand and even more." A serious dislocation of community life was the result: "all business ceased, all craftsmen deserted their crafts. The result was a dreadful famine."

From this period until the eighteenth century plague remained endemic in Europe. The most terrible of all these afflictions was the Black Death of 1347-1348. It made its first appearance in the Crimea, though its breeding ground was probably central Asia. It was brought to Europe by Genoese seamen putting into Messina in Sicily. Both the rate of incidence and of mortality were appalling, so the records show. Many contemporary writers testify to the suddenness of its onset. People walking about the streets, apparently in excellent health, would be struck down without warning. They would hardly be able to creep home, there to die within a short space of time. It has been calculated that a quarter of Europe's population died—no less than twenty-five million people.

The seventeenth century was to see a further outbreak all over Europe. The Great Plague of London of 1664-1665 was part of a much wider epidemic. It was not until the nineteenth century that the brake began to be applied through the advance of preventive medicine. When Edward Jenner discovered vaccination a new era of hope was inaugurated. One by one the great killers were tamed, until today the once dreadful names of cholera and smallpox strike little terror into our minds as we leave the surgery after inoculation. Even as recently, however, as 1918 an influenza epidemic killed in four weeks more than twice as many as the warring armies had destroyed in four years. In the estimation of Charles Singer, lecturer in the history of medicine in the University of London, "disease has always been and still remains the greatest enemy of civilization, and indeed of mankind."

Even in this day of modern drugs, vaccinations and precautionary restrictions, disease has run through scores of countries. Millions die each year from uncontrollable epidemics and incurable complaints. The World Health Organization, established in 1948, has no thought of disbanding on the grounds that its work is done, and continues to combat disease in every part of the earth. Its programme of epidemiological surveillance and eradication is a comprehensive one. In dealing with malaria alone there are five international centres, situated in Lagos, Lomé (Togo), Manila, Maracay (Venezuela), and Sao Paulo (Brazil). A recent report shows that whilst twelve programmes covering 626 million people are making satisfactory progress, twenty-two others covering 230 million people are slow, and eight covering 35 million are very limited in effect.

In addition to the well-known fevers, we hear of some which are quite unfamiliar. Onchocerciasis and dilharziasis are hardly household terms. The first is river blindness caused by microsopic worms transmitted from person to person by blackflies. The second is snail fever caused by blood flukes transmitted by freshwater snails. In tropical countries, these represent a serious menace to health. Within the last few years epidemics of encephalitis and meningitis have killed thousands in China. The more familiar smallpox has raged in India, whilst cholera has presented a dire threat in the past six years. There has been the fear of bubonic plague in Vietnam in the wake of war. The world's rat population is now estimated at 4,800 million, as compared with a human population of 3,353 million (June 1966). Many of these rats carry plague-infested fleas, and there is general concern over their increase.

Disease, then, continues to be one of the signs of our times. Our Lord has assured us that this will be so to the end. It may be that, like the other signs, this too will intensify as the close of the age approaches. Whilst as Christians we range ourselves on the side of all those who seek to rid the earth of disease—and, of course, the missionary Church is deeply involved in this all over the world—we do not expect complete success this side of the millennium. Only then will no inhabitant say, "I am sick" (Is. 33:24); "for I will restore health to you," promises the Lord (Jer. 30:17). The persistence of disease in the world is in itself an indication that the kingdom has not yet fully come. In the sense that they now acknowledge the rule of the King it has already come in Christians. But in society the kingdom still tarries. It awaits the return of Christ. So we sing with Charles Kingsley:—

And hasten, Lord, that perfect day
When pain and death shall cease,
And Thy just rule shall fill the earth
With health, and light, and peace.

Chapter Eleven

POVERTY

ON the eve of what was humanly speaking the greatest adventure in history—the landing on the moon—B.B.C. television presented a special programme in the "Your Witness" series. With Ludovic Kennedy in the chair, John Mortimer proposed the motion "That going to the moon and the planets is not in man's best interests." It was opposed by Quintin Hogg and eventually lost by six votes to twenty-three. It was curious that whereas the humanist John Mortimer called two Christians as witnesses, in the persons of Lord Soper and Nicholas Stacey (deputy director of Oxfam), the Anglican Quintin Hogg relied on the evidence of science and sociology. The argument turned on the enormous expense involved in the moon project and the question as to whether it was justifiable in a world of so much poverty. Of course, no one could prove that had this vast sum of money not been spent on space research it would have been available to help the poor. Further, it may well be that the scientific information gained from visiting the moon and planets will bring such benefits to mankind that even from an economic point of view the venture will ultimately be vindicated.

Whatever we may think about that, the fact of such a debate at such a time emphasizes our current preoccupation with the problem of poverty. Not that there is anything new about the fact of deprivation: it is man's concern which has grown.

Poverty itself has always been with us. That indeed was what Jesus Himself suggested. Immediately after the apocalyptic discourse recorded in Matthew twenty-four and twenty-five, our Lord is found at Bethany in the house of Simon the leper. There a woman came to Him with an alabaster jar filled with some costly unguent, and as He sat at table she began to pour it over His head. It was an act of unparalleled devotion, but when the disciples saw it, they were indignant at the apparent waste. It could have been sold for a tidy sum, as we say, and the proceeds handed over to the poor. Jesus knew just how their minds worked. "Why must you make trouble for the woman?" He asked. "It is a fine thing she has done for me. You have the poor among you always; but you will not always have me. When she poured this oil on my body it was her way of preparing me for burial. I tell you this: wherever in all the world this gospel is proclaimed, what she has done will be told as her memorial" (Matt. 26:10-13 N.E.B.).

Jesus' reply to the niggling criticism of His disciples—John makes Judas their spokesman (John 12:4)—is memorable indeed. "Its originality stamps it as authentic," declared Dr Alfred Plummer. Only Jesus could have said a thing like this. It was almost as if He had implied that, for the time being at least, the poor did not matter. Of course, we know from the rest of His sayings that His attitude was not one of indifference. But what must claim our attention just now is His statement concerning the continuing prevalence of poverty. The poor, He assumed, are ever present. The implication is that they will always be so. There is an echo of Deuteronomy 15:11—"For the poor will never cease out of the land; therefore I command you, You shall open wide your hand to your brother, to the needy, and to the poor, in the land." The comment of the Talmud is: "God allows the poor to be with us for ever, that the opportunities of doing good may never fail."

Poverty is not specifically included amongst the signs of the times mentioned by our Lord in His Olivet seminar. But wherever there is war, famine, earthquake, and disease, poverty is sure to prevail. Certainly the course of history to the present day has confirmed Christ's dictum. Even now, no social factor is more obvious. Whatever ameliorations our scientific age has brought—and we should not underrate them—the shadow of poverty hangs over a large part of our world. We see comparatively little of it in the west though it is there often enough beneath the surface, but no one can tour the east without being appalled by it.

Throughout the New Testament the presence of the poor is reflected as a permanent feature of the community. It is to them that the gospel is preached (Matt. 11:5; Luke 4:18). In our Lord's beatitudes they are the first to be blessed and assured of the kingdom. Luke's version is startling: "Blessed are you poor, for yours is the kingdom of God" (Luke 6:20). In Matthew it becomes "the poor in spirit," and that is no doubt the deeper meaning. It may be that the poor and the pious were virtually synonymous, but that does not remove the fact that they were indeed poor. That Luke was thinking in the first place about economic poverty when he set down this saying of our Lord is indicated in the contrasting woes which follow from v. 24. "But woe to you that are rich, for you have received your consolation." The same interpretative refinement has occurred in the case of the fourth beatitude. In Luke it reads: "Blessed are you that hunger now, for you shall be satisfied" (v. 21). In Matthew it is expanded to: "Blessed are those who hunger and thirst for righteousness" (Matt. 5:6). As A. H. McNeile explained the word *ptochos* "describes the pious in Israel, for the most part literally poor, whom the worldly rich despised and persecuted."

Jesus taught that these must be shown hospitality (Luke 14:12-14) and given alms (Luke 18:22). Their own offerings, though apparently small, might represent sacrificial generosity (Mark 12:41-44). Acts shows this same attitude of concern for the poverty-stricken carried over into the early Church. As a result of the communalism outlined in Acts 2:44, 45 and again in 4:32-37, it could be reported of the Jerusalem believers that "there was not a needy person among them" (Acts 4:34). The war on want within the Christian body itself was waged with complete success, though, of course, conditions in the world around remained the same. Distribution was made on a single principle, which still holds good: "as any had need" (Acts 2:45; 4:35). At first the apostles themselves were the almoners but it was soon necessary to appoint others to undertake this task (Acts 6:1-6). The tables mentioned may have been counters where money was doled out, or meal benches where food was provided. The comment of Professor J. Rawson Lumby bears consideration: "It is deserving of notice that, before we find any special arrangements made for what we now understand by 'divine service', the regulation of the relief of those in need had become so engrossing a part of the duty of the twelve as to have thrust aside in some degree the prayers and ministration of the word, which were especially their charge."

At the end of Acts eleven we read of a remarkable extension of this care for the poor. When Agabus forecast a serious famine in the reign of Claudius, the disciples in Syrian Antioch "determined, every one according to his ability, to send relief to the brethren who lived in Judaea" (Acts 11:29), and this they duly did through Barnabas and Saul. Here was Christian Aid in action, and the really significant feature is that this contribution was made not only from Jewish but from Gentile churches. The apostle Paul speaks of similar aid (e.g. 1 Cor. 16:1-3). In the case of the Macedonian churches, the givers themselves must have been far from affluent, for they had been harshly treated by their Roman conquerors, who exploited their natural resources and reserved for themselves the benefits which accrued from the felling of timber and the mining of salt. Hence it was from the depths of their poverty that they gave "according to their means" and indeed "beyond their means" (2 Cor. 8:3).

One of the issues which is being discussed at present by the exegetes is the degree to which Christian care for the poor may have extended beyond the family of the Church in the apostolic age. Whatever conclusions may be drawn in this respect, it is evident that poverty remained as a continuing factor in society, and this has been so throughout history. Despite all efforts to eradicate the evil—many of them prompted by Christian concern—it still persists, and will do to the end. The war on want has to be carried on unremittingly. In our era we are only too painfully aware that we have the poor always with us.

In this present evil world the "have nots" far outnumber the "haves", and that has been the way of things throughout the centuries. The counterpart of poverty is the concentration of wealth in the hands of the few. This factor is also reflected in the New Testament. The prophets' strictures against the unscrupulous rich are reiterated in the teaching of Jesus. After the young ruler had gone away with a heavy heart, because he was a man of considerable wealth, Jesus turned to His followers and said: "How hard it will be for those who have riches to enter the kingdom of God!" (Mark 10:23). Not unnaturally, the disciples were staggered at such an observation. But our Lord repeated it, and then added graphically: "It is easier for a camel to go through the eye of a needle than for a rich man to enter the kingdom of God" (Mark 10:25). This is a piece of hyperbole "quite in the style of one whose speech sparkled with picturesque comparisons and metaphors," as Professor B. H. Branscomb has noted. We should not allow the wittiness of the saying to obscure its point.

According to James, the rich whose gains are ill-gotten have simply been laying up treasure for the last days (Jas. 5:3). They are to weep and howl for the miseries that are coming upon them (Jas. 5:1). But in the final age, the poor will be vindicated and rewarded. They have laid up treasure in heaven beyond the reach of moth and rust. The persistence of poverty and riches in the world as it now is, constitutes a constant reminder that injustice will not last for ever. In the coming kingdom, all wrongs will be redressed, and the curse of want banished from the face of the earth. Like each of the four freedoms, this liberation from the bondage of poverty will be achieved only when Jesus is King.

Chapter Twelve

IMMORALITY

DAVID FROST'S life is nothing if not varied—
Britain's most controversial television personality
is apt to turn up in all sorts of places. On the
screen we may see him compèring some satirical
late-night revue, or guiding a serious discussion
programme. His interview with Billy Graham was
a classic and is widely used as a film in the interests
of evangelism. He commutes regularly between
London and New York, and here in Britain travels
all round the country on projects of surprising
variety. Not long ago he arrived late with due
apologies to join a B.B.C. *Any Questions?* Team
in Bideford, Devon. He had just flown in a private
plane from East Anglia, where he had been
addressing a Methodist public school on Speech
Day. Within minutes he was involved in a lively
debate about current standards of morality. He
amused the audience by telling them that he had
noticed a huge poster in London bearing this an-
nouncement: "Ten Commandments: Last Week."
It was, of course, outside a cinema, and referred to
a famous film, but the incident was effectively used
to indicate the way things appeared to be going.

On every hand today we hear about the per-
missive society. Moral ideals which have been
cherished for centuries are being questioned and
often jettisoned. The motto of the hour seems to
be "anything goes." Young people are growing
up in an atmosphere of frightening libertarianism.
Immorality has always existed, but it now claims

the support of philosophy and indeed in some cases of religion. Much of what is now taking place is done in the name of a new morality which to many appears to be indistinguishable from the old immorality. We are living in the midst of an ethical revolution.

The new morality is not quite as recent as some imagine. What we are seeing just now is really its second wave. Its genesis may be traced to an essay published by Aldous Huxley as far back as 1929. It was entitled "Fashions in Love," and was simply one of a collection of articles dealing with a number of quite unrelated subjects. Huxley did not actually use the term "new morality," although it was already in circulation. He wrote instead about "the new twentieth-century conception of love," which in his view was then struggling to displace "the conception evolved by the nineteenth century out of the ideals of Christianity on the one hand and romanticism on the other." Bertrand Russell's *Marriage and Morals* appeared in the same year to provide the earliest text-book of the new morality.

In its more recent form, however, the new morality has been supplied with a philosophical basis in what is known as situational ethics. True morality is declared to be the free response of love, unfettered by general rules, to each situation by which it is confronted. This outlook has been adopted even by certain thinkers within the institutional Church, who affirm that nothing is intrinsically evil except the lack of love and, conversely, that where love is present evil becomes good and sin may be excused. Now it is this specious rationalization which is so dangerous today. Man is not naturally inclined to submit to the sanctions of morality, and when these are undermined for him by the intellectual and even some of the religious leaders of the time, he quite understandably assumes that he has a new licence for uninhibited misconduct.

All this apparently unprecedented excess leads many to wonder whether it is an indication that we are now approaching the end of the age. It is assumed that the moral condition of the world is worse than it has ever been, and that therefore we must be hastening to the final destruction. It is common to appeal to Scripture to substantiate the thesis that iniquity will increase as the return of Christ draws nearer, and there are some passages which may seem to suggest it. But viewed in overall perspective, the Bible more certainly asserts that immorality is a mark of every age. In other words, it is a sign of the times—those times which run throughout the Christian era. It may also be a sign of the end, but the mere fact that iniquity abounds today does not necessarily imply that the last things are almost upon us. It may abound yet more before the end. Our Lord declared that wickedness will be multiplied, but who can tell when its cup is full? (Matt. 24:12).

One of the most devastating descriptions of human degeneration is to be found in the third chapter of Second Timothy. Here is how *Living Letters* paraphrases it: "People will love only themselves and their money; they will be proud and boastful, sneering at God, disobedient to their parents, ungrateful to them, and thoroughly bad. They will be hardhearted and never give in to others; they will be constant liars and troublemakers and will think nothing of immorality. They will be rough and cruel, and sneer at those who try to be good. They will betray their friends; they will be hot-headed, puffed up with pride, and prefer good times to worshipping God" (2 Tim. 3:2-4). How up-to-date it all sounds! That is just our generation, we say. And, of course, it is. Then we glance back to v. 1 and read that all this belongs to "the last days," when times of stress will come for Christians. But we have already explained that in the New Testament "the last days" are not the same as "the last day." They cover the whole period from the ascension to the return of our Lord. The sort of immorality depicted here is typical of other ages as well as of our own.

To realize that we only have to thumb back in our Bible to the latter half of Romans one. From verse 18 Paul proceeds to expose the exceeding sinfulness of sin. He goes into all the sordid details of sexual excess and perversion, and winds up with a catalogue of enormities in verses 29 to 31 which may be set side by side with those in 2 Timothy 3:2-4. But the tense of the verbs throughout is in the past. The apostle is speaking of what has been happening in his own time. Only in v. 32 does he revert to the present to show that it is still going on. Immorality, then, is a feature of every generation and not just of the last. There are similar references in 2 Peter 2:12-14 ("eyes full of adultery, insatiable for sin") and v. 18 ("they entice with licentious passions of the flesh men who have barely escaped from those who live in error"). In these same "last days," scoffers will arise "following their own passions," and querying the reality of the second advent (2 Peter 3:3, 4).

Later in the Olivet discourse, Jesus spoke about the time before the flood and compared it with that which will precede His own return. "As were the days of Noah, so will be the coming of the Son of man" (Matt. 24:37). It has been fashionable to stress that the antediluvian era was one of inordinate wickedness, and to conclude that the same conditions will prevail immediately prior to the end. But whilst this may prove to be so, it is not the point our Lord desired to make. What men and women were doing was to eat and drink, to marry and give in marriage. There is nothing immoral about that. These are normal, neutral preoccupations. It is only when God's warnings are taken into consideration that they acquire a sinister significance. God had given these men an interval of grace, and yet they immersed themselves in the things of this life as though no judgment were impending. That was their offence. As a result, the flood descended upon them unawares and swept them all away. That is how it will be when the Son of man returns. It is not that men everywhere will be engaged in some orgy of unspeakable depravity. Most of them will be about the customary affairs of life, heedless of every admonition. As Professor R. C. H. Lenski brings out in his comment on this passage, it is not the wickedness of immorality that Jesus emphasises but negligent blindness. "They did not know" (Matt. 24:39)—but they should have known. That was how it was before the flood. That is how it will be before the Lord's return.

The immorality which typifies succeeding ages of history is itself an expression of antipathy to God. It is the outcome of what the New Testament calls *anomia*, or lawlessness—a revolt against authority of every kind. It is the ultimate anarchy. Where there is no vision of God, the people cast off restraint. (Prov. 29:18). Joseph Butler, Bishop of Bristol and author of the famous *Analogy of*

Religion, described the climate of the eighteenth century as "truly *for* nothing, but against everything that is good and sacred among us." That is the essence of *anomia*. It overthrows existing structures of morality, but is incapable of erecting anything in their place. It is the direct result of denying God. Morality depends on Him. Ours is an age without standards because it is an age without God. Those standards survived for a while when divorced from their source, but only for a while. Like the grin which lingered on when the Cheshire cat had vanished, they cannot last. It was Jean-Paul Sartre, the existentialist, who had the discernment to declare: "If God is not, everything is changed and everything is allowed." That is how it is today and in every age which thinks it can dispense with God.

It would be a sad surrender if the Church were to give up the good fight in our time on the ground that abounding iniquity at the end is inevitable. Our gospel reminds us that where sin increases, grace immeasurably exceeds it (Rom. 5:20). Nothing is impossible with God. We are not to knuckle under to the current predominance of evil. In the name of Christ we must do battle against it. We are to "meet the sons of night," and "mock their vain design." "A counter-reformation in ethics is long overdue," declares Professor C. A. Campbell of Glasgow. How right he is! Christians must lead it. And they must recognize that it can be brought about only by the gospel. New conduct demands new men, and men can be made new in no other way than by Christ.

Chapter Thirteen

APOSTASY

A regular feature of the *Reader's Digest* is a quiz entitled "It Pays to Increase Your Word Power." The caption certainly represents a truth for Christians. It is an advantage to be familiar with the Word of God. This is the sword of the Spirit which we must learn to wield with dexterity and skill. Such expertise will involve a knowledge not only of the biblical content in general, but of its vocabulary in particular. Those who believe that the Scriptures are verbally inspired are under an especial obligation to examine the words within the Word with exceptional care.

The biographer of John Henry Jowett reveals that if that great preacher had any hobby it was the study of words. He loved to take a word, as an entomologist takes a moth, and having (figuratively speaking) stuck a pin through it, to subject it to a long microscopic examination. One day Jowett's friend, Edgar Todd, out walking with him in Sutton Park, wanted to show him how the Holly Blue butterfly differs from the Common Blue. With the utmost caution he approached the resting insect, so that he could lift it off the leaf without injury to show the marking on the underside of the wings. Dr Jowett watched in fascinated silence. When the operation was completed, he said: "That is just how I pick up a word."

It is with such consummate care that the Bible student should pick up each word of Scripture in order to discover its exact significance. Much misinterpretation in the past has stemmed from insufficient attention to semantics. Happily today we are better equipped than ever before to undertake such research, for the several volumes of Gerhard Kittel's monumental *Theologisches Wörterbuch zum Neuen Testament* (A Theological Dictionary of the New Testament) are open to consultation and are now being done into English.

The term "apostasy," with which we are concerned in this chapter, is derived directly from the Greek *apostasia*. It denotes the state of apostasy, as distinct from the act of apostatising which is covered by a cognate noun. In classical literature it originally referred to deserting a post or station in life. It is used by Plutarch and others of political revolt. It occurs in this sense in the Septuagint, but there the allusion is more often to religious rebellion. In Joshua 22:22 the Reubenites, Gadites and the half-tribe of Manasseh say to the captains of Israel: "God, even God, is the Lord, and God even God himself knows, and Israel shall know: if we have transgressed against the Lord by way of rebellion, do not deliver us today." "Your wickedness will chasten you, and your apostasy will reprove you," the Lord announces in Jeremiah 2:19. "Know and see that it is evil and bitter for you to forsake the Lord your God." 2 Chronicles 29:19 refers to the faithlessness of Ahaz, and 33:19 to that of Manasseh. In the First Book of Maccabees 2:15 we learn how Antiochus Epiphanes enforced an apostasy from Judaism to Hellenism.

In the New Testament, the reproach is brought against Paul that he taught the Jews "to forsake Moses" (Acts 21:21), by advising them not to have their children circumcised nor to observe cere-

monial customs now that they were Christians.
The New English Bible has "to turn their backs
on Moses." It meant the rejection of the law. The
same term is applied to Christians, if they fall away
from their faith and lapse into error and un-
righteousness. Hermann Cremer states that *apostasia*
is employed in the absolute sense of "passing over
to unbelief," and thus involves a dissolution of the
"union with God subsisting through faith in
Christ." It is the utter abandonment of any
attachment to the Lord.

In His apocalyptic discourse on the mount of
Olives, Jesus anticipated such defections. "And
then many will fall away," He said, "and betray
one another, and hate one another" (Matt. 24:10).
The verb there is *skandalizō*—to stumble. Here it
is in the passive form—to be made to stumble.
The noun *skandalon* really means the bait-stick of
a mousetrap. Many will be caught like this, so
Jesus prophesied, during the course of the centuries
and right up to His return. The apostle Paul was
aware of the same possibility. "Now the Spirit
expressly says that in later times some will depart
from the faith"—and the verb is "apostatize."
(1 Tim. 4:1). In his farewell to the Ephesian
elders, Paul had spoken of this. "I know that after my
departure fierce wolves will come in among you,
not sparing the flock; and from among your own
selves will arise men speaking perverse things, to
draw away the disciples after them" (Acts 20:29,
30). And writing to the believers in Colosse he
warned: "See to it that no one makes a prey of
you by philosophy and empty deceit, according to
human tradition" (Col. 2:8). Jesus Himself had
spoken about the seed dropped on the rock, which

represented those who have no root and who fall away in the time of testing (Luke 8:13).

The New Testament itself provides some pathetic instances of such defection. There were Hymenaeus and Alexander who, with others, "made shipwreck of their faith" (1 Tim. 1:19). There were Phygelus and Hermogenes, who turned away from Paul, and perhaps from Christ as well (2 Tim. 1:15). There was Demas the deserter, who was "in love with this present world" (2 Tim. 4:10). There are those who had escaped from the defilements of the world through the knowledge of Christ, who were "again entangled in them and overpowered," so that "the last state has become worse for them than the first" (2 Peter 2:20). There are those of whom John writes that "they went out from us, but they were not of us; for if they had been of us, they would have continued with us; but they went out, that it might be plain that they all are not of us" (1 John 2:19). Hence the injuction of Hebrews 3:12—"Take care, brethren, lest there be in any of you an evil, unbelieving heart, leading you to fall away from the living God."

The doctrinal content of this apostasy is sufficiently indicated in the New Testament letters. It is specifically described as a defection from the faith (1 Tim. 4:1). There is a body of apostolic truth to which the Christian gives his allegiance. To deny it is to apostatize. Such defecters "will not endure sound teaching," and "turn away from listtning to the truth" (2 Tim. 4:3,4). They prefer myths ingeniously invented by clever men (2 Peter 1:16). They reject authority (Jude 8). They disown the Lordship of Christ as they import their destructive heresies (2 Peter 2:1). They refuse to confess Him as of God (1 John 4:3). They query the second coming (2 Peter 3:4). They deny the resurrection (1 Cor. 15:12). They are "men of corrupt mind and counterfeit faith" who "preserve the outward form of religion, but are a standing denial of its reality" (2 Tim. 3:8; 3:5 N.E.B.). We are only too familiar with these marks of apostasy today. Russell Kirk, in *The Intemperate Professor*, refers to those who have discarded Christian theology "like so much antiquated rubbish."

This is bad enough when it is done in the name of agnosticism. It is even worse when the label of Christianity is still retained. There is an apostasy which pretends not to fall away overtly. It maintains itself inside the framework of the institutional Church. It constitutes a rebellion within. This is when apostasy is manifested in its most dangerous form. The death of God theology, so much in vogue at present, falls into this category. Its progenitor was the cynical atheist Friedrich Nietzsche, and we are not surprised that men of his outlook should speak in such terms. But that those who represent, or claim to represent, the mind of the Church should talk about the death of God is the ultimate blasphemy. Of course, not all who use this terminology mean by it that God can be written off, but some appear to do so. Dr James Packer has said that much of the current advocacy on behalf of "religionless Christianity" reminds him of an advertizement he once saw as a schoolboy. It ran: "For Sale: a bladeless knife without a handle."

Whilst such a falling away is to be expected to some degree in every age of the Church, and has in fact proved to be a sadly recurring feature, there is one New Testament passage which unambiguously speaks about an apostasy at the end which is so horrendous as to require the definite article. It is *the* apostasy. In 2 Thessalonians 2:3 Paul writes: "For that day will not come unless the rebellion (*apostasia*) comes first." The New English Bible has "final rebellion." The Jerusalem Bible makes it "the Great Revolt," and J. B. Phillips "a definite rejection of God." "That day" is identified as "the day of the Lord" in v. 2. In the First Letter Paul has written about the Lord's return and the need to be ready for it (1 Thess. 2:19; 5:1-11). He has also mentioned the Christian's "assembling to meet him" in the rapture (2 Thess. 2:1; 1 Thess. 4:13-18). Now he indicates what must first occur, lest his readers should be deceived (2 Thess. 2:3). There had been a period of apostasy before Christ's first coming, when Antiochus Epiphanes had seduced many Jews from the faith. There will evidently be a similar period of apostasy before Christ's second coming. Paul proceeds to depict it in the verses which follow. The man of lawlessness will be revealed. He is the very incarnation of *anomia*. He is the son of perdition, the Enemy (N.E.B.), who exalts himself as God. He is the apotheosis of apostasy.

To learn who he is we have to compare this passage with the Book of Daniel. (cf. 7:25; 8:4, 9-14, 25, 26). He is the antichrist. It is he who denies both the Father and the Son (1 John 2:22). In him the last rebellion finds its focus and its head. Dr Harold Ockenga, recently appointed President of Gordon Divinity School, is not given to rash, unfounded speculations. Perhaps we ought to ponder his comment: "In this present great apostasy from New Testament Christianity we could see a sign which will warrant us in believing that Christ's coming may not be far away. There has always been some measure of apostasy and at times that apostasy has been great, but not as it has been in the last fifty years."

Chapter Fourteen

CULTS

ANY day a knock or a ring will announce that a representative of one of the modern religious cults is seeking to interest us in his line of patter. Once his foot is over the threshold, we may be in for a lengthy session, and if we do not resist there will be offers of literature and even the playing of gramophone records or tapes. The Englishman's traditional castle is under attack: few homes to-day are invulnerable. And where persistent visits fail, radio may succeed, for a casual twiddling of the wavelength knob may inadvertently bring one of the programmes they put out. We live in an age of cults.

"The rise and development of the heresies current throughout the world today," according to Oswald Sanders, until recently General Director of the Overseas Missionary Fellowship, "constitutes one of the most remarkable features of contemporary religious history." There never was a time when so many flourished; their growth during the present century has been little short of phenomenal. In the United States of America they spawn like tadpoles and quickly emerge as raucously vocal frogs. Great Britain has felt their impact more forcibly in recent years. On the continent of Africa and in the east they find a happy hunting ground. These Christian deviations, as Professor Horton Davies rightly describes them, are a sign of the times.

The Scriptures lead us to expect this; there are

enough warnings in the New Testament to put us on our guard against the menace of the cults. Jesus Himself said in the Sermon on the Mount: "Beware of false prophets, who come to you in sheep's clothing but inwardly are ravenous wolves. You will know them by their fruits. Are grapes gathered from thorns, or figs from thistles? So, every sound tree bears good fruit, but the bad tree bears evil fruit" (Matt. 7:15-17). To expect genuine spiritual benefit from one of these off-centre cults is like looking for ripe fruit on a rotten tree. In the Olivet discourse concerning the future course of history, Jesus repeated His admonition. Immediately after referring to apostasy, He added: "And many false prophets will arise and lead many astray" (Matt. 24:11). Already in verse 5 He had stressed the same thing. Indeed the first words of His address to the disciples are these: "Take heed that no one leads you astray. For many will come in my name, saying, 'I am the Christ,' and they will lead many astray" (Matt. 24:4, 5). In Mark, the implications of Matthew 24:11 are drawn out more fully. "False Christs and false prophets will arise and show signs and wonders, to lead astray, if possible, the elect. But take heed; I have told you all things beforehand" (Mark 13:22, 23).

The apostle Paul was unequivocal in his denunciation of such false teachers. "There are some who trouble you and want to pervert the gospel of Christ," he tells the Galatians. "But even if we, or an angel from heaven, should preach to you a gospel contrary to that which we preached to you, let him be accursed" (Gal. 1:7, 8). And again, writing to Titus: "For there are many insubordinate men, empty talkers and deceivers, especially the circumcision party; they must be silenced, since they are upsetting whole families by teaching for base gain what they have no right to teach" (Titus 1:10, 11). Peter is equally emphatic: "There will be false teachers among you, who will secretly bring in destructive heresies, even denying the Master who bought them, bringing upon themselves swift destruction. And many will follow their licentiousness, and because of them the way of truth will be reviled" (2 Peter 2:1, 2). There is a similar reference in Jude 4.

One of the most relevant passages is to be found in 1 Timothy 4:1-5. Here we learn how cults originate. They are a consequence of apostasy. When men fall away from Christian belief, this is where many of them finish up. They do not all lapse into paganism. They are more likely to get involved in one of the heretical sects. If a Gallup Poll could be taken of these groups today, it would be discovered that a high proportion of their adherents were once members of the Christian Church. Their success in gaining converts from the ranks of unbelievers is comparatively small. "Now the Spirit expressly says that in later times some will depart from the faith by giving heed to deceitful spirits and doctrines of demons, through the pretensions of liars whose consciences are seared" (1 Tim. 4:1, 2). Here is the anatomy of deviation. It is the work of evil spirits. They are agents in the hand of "the spirit of error," or seduction (1 John 4:6). Satan is the father of lies, and it is he who manipulates this "spirit of error" which always and everywhere opposes "the spirit of truth" (1 John 4:6). These subversive doctrines, then, are inspired by demons. The spirits are described as being "deceitful". The adjective really means that they wander. It is the same word in

Greek as that from which we get our "planet". Planets are heavenly bodies distinguished from fixed stars because they have a motion of their own. They wander, as it were, amongst the constellations. These evil spirits are wanderers like that —and they make others wanderers too.

The leaders of heretical cults are pictured as brazen liars who deal in specious falsehoods with never a twinge of conscience because they are past all moral feeling. This is a devastating indictment of such men and their methods, but the case history of cult directors provides enough instances to vindicate it. As Taylor paraphrases it, "these teachers will tell lies with straight faces and do it so often that their consciences won't even bother them." The word translated as "seared" in R.S.V. is really "cauterized." That is a medical term for a process which makes an organ insensitive and callous. The conscience of these religious mountebanks has gone numb. By constant stifling and ignoring of its counsel, it has suffered atrophy. It no longer functions. The Spirit has not only been grieved and resisted, but actually quenched. This is what happened to Balaam. He was so desensitized that for a suitable fee he was quite prepared to put a curse on God's chosen people. Another interpretation of the same expression is that these spiritual charlatans have been branded like slaves or criminals. That is how the New English Bible takes it. The devil has put his own sign upon them. They are marked out unmistakeably as his.

From verse 6 onwards Paul tells Timothy how he should deal with such heresy. "Have nothing to do with godless and silly myths" (v. 7). Such profane drivel, "fit only for old women" (N.E.B.), is to be shunned. It may purport to deal with religious themes but it possesses no religious value. It may often talk about God, but it is actually godless since it spurns the Christian revelation. It rests on myths rather than truth. A leading article in a national newspaper recently regretted what it called the "Kennedy mythomania" of the American people. The comment was prompted by the misgivings aroused by the car accident in which Senator Edward Kennedy was involved, with tragic loss of life. "Mythomania" is a suitable and scriptural description of cult heresy.

The reference to the forbidding of marriage and the encouragement of fasting suggests that the particular form of deviation Paul had in mind here was that which developed in the second century into the complex of ideas and practices known as Gnosticism. It represents one of two main streams which have given rise to the present day cults, the other being the Judaistic perversion of the Christian faith. The Gnostic tendency has been towards religious eclecticism and the fusing of Christian and non-Christian elements in a kind of anthology. Examples of this type persisting today are Theosophy, Spiritism, Swedenborgianism and Christian Science. The Judaistic heresies are represented by Seventh Day Adventism, Jehovah's Witnesses, British Israel, Christadelphianism, and Mormonism.

Professor Horton Davies lists some of the perils involved in cultism, so that Christians may be on their guard against them. 1. The danger of mistaking the part for the whole in Christian faith or practice. 2. The danger of an over-emphasis on the Old Testament to the detriment of the New. 3. The danger of confusing Christianity with pantheism. 4. The danger of seeking for greater assurance in the religious life than Christ offers. 5. The danger of spiritual pride, issuing in schismatic exclusivism or intellectual snobbery. 6. The danger of using God as a means to an end. 7. The danger of an individualistic pietism which renounces social responsibilities. 8. The supreme danger of failing to acknowledge the fulness, the uniqueness, and the finality of the Christian doctrine of the Incarnation. The first seven are apparent in this cult or that, but the last is a common defect in them all. We shall be well advised to watch out for these danger signals within the Christian community itself, in addition to recognizing them as the trademarks of deviationism.

Such, then, is what J. K. Van Baalen has called "the chaos of the cults" Their very confusion is evidence of their origin. Ours is not a God of disorder but of harmony (1 Cor. 14:33). We seem to be living in one of the "later times" of which Paul speaks, when such heresies abound (1 Tim. 4:1). The only antidote is "the sound words of our Lord Jesus Christ and the teaching which accords with godliness," which the apostle recommends (1 Tim. 6:3). Those who stray from it themselves, and lead others into their error, "have let their reasoning powers become atrophied and have lost grip of the truth" (1 Tim. 6:5 N.E.B.). The man of God will have nothing to do with such deceit. He will echo the bold resolve of Isaac Watts:

> Should all the forms that men devise
> Assault my faith with treacherous art,
> I'd call them vanity and lies,
> And bind Thy gospel to my heart.

Chapter Fifteen

WORLDLINESS

THE evangelist Tom Rees recalls that when he was a young Christian the Lord gave him a strange counsellor in spiritual things. This was a hermit who lived in the Whippendale woods, coming into Watford on Saturdays to sell his wares. There Tom Rees first met him. He was a Christian of remarkable maturity, and they soon struck up a friendship. Each week Tom would look forward to a long talk with him. One Saturday evening, the recluse called Tom to him and said something which has always remained with him. It was this: "A ship is all right in the sea, but if the sea gets into the ship, the ship sinks. A Christian is all right in the world, but if the world gets into the Christian, the Christian sinks."

The neccessity of separation from the world must always be impressed upon converts at the very beginning. This is where holiness starts: a false step early on can stultify the whole Christian life. We must resolve our attitude to the world or our effectiveness in service may be jeopardized. "We are separated first," writes Dr Wilbur Smith, "then we partake of new life; we belong to God, then we are to live for God." The teaching of Scripture on this crucial issue is summarized in I John 2:15-17. "Do not love the world or the things in the world. If any one loves the world, love for the Father is not in him. For all that is in the world, the lust of the flesh and the lust of the eyes and the pride of life, is not of the Father but is of the world.

And the world passes away, and the lust of it; but he who does the will of God abides for ever."

Since worldliness is a problem for the believer it must also be one for the Church, for the Church is simply the fellowship of believers. What we read in the New Testament leads us to expect that the temptation to be conformed to this world will pester the Christian and endanger the Church throughout the course of history. Some believe that this tendency will be intensified as the close of the age approaches. However this may be, Christians today certainly feel the pull of worldliness to be unusually strong. There are saddening indications that too often the Church is guilty of succumbing. The Church must needs be in the world, as we are continually reminded by contemporary theologians; but when the world gets into the Church, there is the danger of betrayal.

Commenting on the scene earlier in this present decade, the late Dean Samuel H. Miller of Harvard complained: "The Church simply does not have a cutting edge. It has taken the culture of our time and absorbed it. The Church is run, not to serve the reality of human beings but to conserve institutions." Some may consider this indictment too sweeping, but it can hardly be denied that there is enough truth in it to make us pause. That this is no innovation is borne out by the observations of Sir Herbert Butterfield in his *Christianity and History*. He attributes the beginning of this process to the liaison between Church and State in the time of Constantine. It has continued to our own day. "By its alliance with power for fifteen hundred years, the Church committed itself to being on the whole the cement of society, the buttress of whatever was the existing order, and the defender of the *status quo*—at one time thinking that its interests were bound up with absolute monarchy, at another time clinging to a form of aristocracy, with all the fervour with which we might now expect it to cling to liberal democracy. Indeed almost from the earliest days of that alliance one can hardly read the story without the most serious misgivings, and within the Church itself we are presented with ... the problem of human nature in history. During those fifteen hundred years its leaders were too often the conscious accomplices in things that we deplore today, and much more often still they engaged in those unconscious complicities which always arise when there is an alliance with power, or else they were engaged in the game of power themselves. The story of Protestantism is not in this respect structurally different from the story of Roman Catholicism." Professor Butterfield himself believes that in our time the Church is beginning at long last to extricate itself from these political entanglements.

Whilst this may indeed be true in some instances so far as the interrelation of Church and State is concerned, the broader inroads of worldliness do not appear to be mitigated. The continuing temptation of the Church is to align itself with secular influences and conform to the pattern of the times. There is never much future in that, for as Dean Inge once remarked in his epigrammatic way, the Church which is wedded to the spirit of the age in one generation is apt to find itself a widow in the next! The Church has always been at its strongest and most successful when it has refused to make concessions to the conventional standards of the time, but has sought to maintain its own integrity. It may be that a similar period of testing will give it once again an opportunity to rise above the cultural decadence by which it is surrounded, and assert its highest influence. Unless it does, its prospects as an institution can hardly be bright.

It was one of the medieval popes who was once proudly displaying the treasures of the Vatican to a visitor. As he moved from one priceless object to another, he remarked that the Church need no longer say "Silver and gold have I none." "No," replied the other with rare discernment, "and neither can she say 'In the name of Jesus Christ of Nazareth, rise up and walk.'" In amassing temporal resources, the Church had forfeited spiritual power, and that is what always happens when worldliness prevails.

The verb translated as "love" in 1 John 2:15 is one which indicates deliberate choice rather than natural, friendly affection. That is why the New English Bible has "Do not set your hearts on the godless world or anything in it." It needs to be understood that *kosmos* has a number of meanings in the New Testament. It can refer to the universe, to the earth, to the whole human race, to the ungodly, or in the ethical sense to all that is opposed to Christ on earth. Here it seems to be a combination of the last two. It is, as Professor C. H. Dodd puts it, "pagan society, with its sensuality, superficiality and pretentiousness, its materialism and its egoism." John hints at its nature when he speaks about "the lust of the flesh and the lust of the eyes and the pride of life" (1 John 2:16). These are the marks of that old, bad order out of which the Christian has been brought, Dodd explains, into the new order inaugurated by Christ. If a man still hankers after the world, then it is plain that the

Father's love is not in him. That is a simple, undeniable fact. John means something more than that "love for the Father is not in him" (RSV). The genitive is subjective. God's own love, shed abroad in the believer's heart by the Holy Spirit, no longer remains in him. "If a man loves me, he will keep my word," said Jesus, "and my Father will love him, and we will come to him and make our home with him." (John 14:23). Anyone who retains his former love for the world, prevents the love of God from dwelling in his heart. This is the nemesis of worldliness.

The reason why the Christian cannot have any truck with the world if he is to survive spiritually is that it is evanescent. "The world passes away, and the lust of it" (1 John 2:17). As Paul told the Corinthians, "the form of this world is passing away" (1 Cor. 7:31). It is transient. It is its very nature not to last. Every day its doom is overtaking it. As Lenski dramatically asks: "The bank is breaking, it was never solvent—will you deposit in it? The foundation is tottering, it was never solid but only sham—will you build on it? The mountain is rumbling, quaking, it was never anything but volcanic, ready to blow off its head at any time—will you build your city there?" That is how the Christian must needs regard the world. Then, in sudden, striking contrast, John adds firmly: "but he who does the will of God abides for ever" (1 John 2:17).

We hear a great deal just now from the radical theologians about what they call "worldly religion" and the "secular gospel." Insofar as it represents a genuine attempt to relate the principle of the Incarnation to the task of mission, this may be legitimate. But if in any sense it results in a conformity to the world's standards on the part of the Church, it is to be rigorously eschewed. Of course the Church must be involved in society, but only in such a way that it is clear beyond all shadow of hesitation that it does not subscribe to the attitudes which prevail there. Incidentally, the question of worldliness will solve itself when the Christian goes among men with his colours nailed bravely to the mast. The man who is in most peril from the world is the man who fails to witness in it. The true believer will not be afraid to do so whilst all the time he is sustained by the resources of the Spirit.

The naturalists tell us that in South America there is a curious little spider which has its home under the water. It forms a bubble about itself in which, like a diving bell, it sinks to the bottom of a pond or a river. It will remain there for hours, living below, and yet breathing the air from above. When it returns to the surface it is found to be perfectly dry. Not the slightest moisture will have penetrated its capsule. It is in the water and yet separate from it, maintained by contact with the beyond.

That is a parable of the Christian life. It is the only secret of survival both for the individual and the Church. That is why Jesus could say of His disciples that they were not of the world, even as He was not of the world. His prayer for us in heaven even now is not that we should be taken out of the world, but that we should be kept from the Evil One.

Chapter Sixteen

PERSECUTION

THE name of Richard Wurmbrandt is known all over the Christian world today. He is the Rumanian pastor who survived fourteen years in Communist prisons, where he suffered unspeakable physical and mental tortures. To hear him tell his story is an unforgettable experience. He will unloose his shirt buttons to show the scars on his body—the marks of the Lord Jesus indeed. Wurmbrandt has become a new John the Baptist, so it has been said, a voice crying in the wilderness on behalf of the underground Church in Eastern Europe. He is a contemporary witness to the fact that the age of persecution is not past. "Here is Christ's mystical body, the real Church," he wrote concerning his fellow believers behind the iron curtain, "which is ready to suffer as her Master for the glory of God and the good of mankind."

The Church will always be under fire. It is permanently up against it. With varying pressures, this has been the situation in every century. The Church was designed to be on the receiving end, as we say, of repressive and hostile treatment. If ever it settled down and found life easy, it would cease to be the Church. Sometimes that has happened to the institution: it can never happen to the true body of Christ. It was destined to be the target of attack. If it were not, it would need to question its identity.

Persecution is one of the signs of the times foretold by our Lord in His apocalyptic discourse.

"They will deliver you up to tribulation, and put you to death," He warned His disciples; "and you will be hated by all nations for my name's sake" (Matt. 24:9). Mark's version is fuller. 'But take heed to yourselves; for they will deliver you up to councils; and you will be beaten in synagogues; and you will stand before governors and kings for my sake, to bear testimony before them" (Mark 13:9). Words could hardly have been plainer than that, nor could they have been more exactly fulfilled even in the apostolic age itself. For, like the other signs we have been considering, this one was clearly characteristic of the earliest years of the Church. Even before the fall of Jerusalem, of which the Olivet address speaks in the first place, persecution had set in. "Remember the word that I said to you, 'A servant is not greater than his master.' If they persecuted me, they will persecute you" (John 15:20).

The initial pressure was applied not by the Romans but by the Jews. The civil authorities in the empire did not appreciate the difference between Christianity and Judaism in the days when the Church was very young, and as a result, Christianity shared the privilege of being a tolerated religion. It was from the Jews that the earliest persecutions came. It is noticeable that Jesus spoke about the disciples being handed over to the courts and flogged in synagogues before He went on to refer to their appearance before governors and kings. That was precisely the order of events. The councils were the minor Jewish courts, in which twenty-three judges sat together to try cases. These councils could decree scourging with rods as a punishment, and this would be carried out in the local synagogue, where the council sat, and under the surveillance of the judges. This was the means by which Saul of Tarsus had brought Christians to book before his dramatic conversion on the Damascus road (Acts 22:19; 26:11). But soon he was to stand with the followers of Jesus as a victim of such flaying (2 Cor. 11:25).

Immediately after the first recorded preaching of the gospel following Pentecost, the apostles were committed to prison for the night (Acts 4:3). They were quickly discharged on this occasion, but before long they were back again and this time they were flogged (Acts 5:40). Stephen was stoned (Acts 7:58). James was killed by Herod Agrippa I (Acts 12:2). This was a period of violent persecution for the Jerusalem church. Throughout his missionary journeys, Paul encountered the fiercest opposition from the Jews; they were for ever stirring up trouble against him.

From the Jewish tribunals, our Lord turns to the pagan courts which were presided over by governors or procurators, and even on occasion by kings. The Herods boasted the latter title, even though they were only tetrarchs. Archelaus is called "the ethnarch" on his coins. The governors included men like Felix and Festus, and perhaps also proconsuls such as Sergius Paulus and Gallio (Acts 23:24; 24:27; 13:7, 8, 12; 18:12; 19:38). Before the fall of Jerusalem, the Roman authorities began to realize that the Christians were not merely a Jewish sect, and that their claim that Christ was supreme even over the emperor constituted a threat to the State. It was for this reason that persecution was intensified, coming to a head in the dreadful pogrom under Nero. The cruelties inflicted on them were well-nigh beyond description. Some were wrapped in the skins of wild beasts, so that they would be more savagely attacked by dogs. Some were smeared with tar and set on fire to make living torches. Some were put to death by crucifixion. The "killing time" for the Church had begun with a vengeance.

It was to continue with mounting severity for two centuries and more. Ten great persecutions succeeded one another, until the reign of the Christian emperor Constantine brought the onslaughts to an end. Christians were indeed "hated by all nations" for the sake of Christ (Matt. 24:9). Tacitus regarded them as "men of the worst character, deserving of extreme and exemplary punishment." To confess to being a Christian was in itself a proof of guilt. As Dr H. B. Workman concluded in his fascinating study of *Persecution in the Early Church*, "the Christians were punished, not as members of an illicit sodality, but 'for the Name'" "What a fool you are," said Maximus the judge to the veteran Julius, "to make more of a crucified man than of living emperors." "He died for our sins that He might give us eternal life," replied the martyr. "Sacrifice and live, then," retorted Maximus. "If I choose life," declared Julius, in a memorable testimony, "I choose death; if I die, I live for ever." Christ or Caesar was the clear-cut issue. The State demanded submission to Caesar; the Christian could yield only to Christ. It was for His name's sake that thousands were put to death.

Persecution is a continuing sign of the times until the Lord's return. There has never been an age when somewhere in the world Christians have not been suffering for their faith. The price of loyalty has been paid in blood. Yet all this has turned out rather to the furtherance of the gospel. No multiplication of external restrictions, or of violent attacks, has succeeded in staying the advance of the truth. Messengers may be flung into prison, and even put to death, but the Word of God is not bound, nor can its life be extinguished. Justin Martyr compared the Church to a vine: the more it bleeds under the pruning-knife of affliction, the more fruitful it becomes. "The more men multiply our sufferings, the more does the number of the faithful grow." And in a celebrated passage, Tertullian could affirm: "The blood of the martyrs is the seed (of the Church). Dying we conquer. The moment we are crushed, that moment we go forth victorious."

The Scriptures promise no immunity from persecution as long as the Church is on the earth. This sign of the times will persist to the end. "Indeed all who desire to live a godly life in Christ Jesus will be persecuted" (2 Tim. 3:12). This is what the Christian must expect. Those who may not be called upon to face the firing squad or the concentration camp, will nevertheless be confronted with the world's hatred. The weapon of ridicule claims its conquests for the power of evil as well as the rack and the thumbscrew. There are Christians today who are in danger of being sneered out of their allegiance to the Master, for the snide remark and the jocular jibe can test the faith of believers as fully as the more obvious instruments of torture. In a day like ours, when the climate of conventional opinion is altogether inimical to the gospel, persecution may make the mind its target rather than the body. How essential it is for us to rely on the Lord to supply us with just the right sort of answer to all the probing questions with which we are plied. We can legitimately interpret our Lord's words in

Mark 13:11 as being relevant to such a situation. "Do not be anxious beforehand what you are to say; but say whatever is give you in that hour, for it is not you who speak, but the Holy Spirit."

However fierce may be the attacks of the enemy, we have an infallible assurance that the Church will not succumb to persecution. Not even the gates of Hades itself can prevail against it. That is the conviction which enables us to endure every test and trial. Victory is certain.

> See the Gospel Church secure,
>   And founded on a rock;
> All her promises are sure;
>   Her bulwarks who can shock?
> Count her every precious shrine;
>   'Tell, to after-ages, tell,
> Fortified by power divine,
>   The Church can never fail
>   (Charles Wesley).

The French reformer, Theodore Beza, made a famous retort to King Henry of Navarre. "Sire, it is truly the lot of the Church of God, for which I speak, to endure blows and not to strike them. But may it please you to remember that it is an anvil which has worn out many hammers."

Chapter Seventeen

EXPANSION

In an interview given shortly before his death, the distinguished historian Professor Kenneth Scott Latourette of Yale was asked a pertinent question. "You have always thought of Christianity in global terms. How do you calculate the impact of Christianity and of Christ upon our generation?" The reply may surprise some. "I am convinced," said Latourette, "that Christ has never been as widely and deeply influential in the world-scene as He is today." These are heartening words for those who have to contend for the faith in what we often take to be unpropitious times. Despite the setbacks, the world mission of the Church is in fact being implemented, and in many areas is gaining ground.

The number of Christians is on the increase, even though it may not always be keeping pace with the population explosion. For example, believers in India fifty years ago represented only one per cent of the inhabitants of that sub-continent. Now the figure is approaching three per cent, and in the same period the total population has risen from 300 million to over 500 million. Here, then, is an instance of growth which is outstripping the birthrate. In Africa south of the Sahara the expansion is probably even greater. Indonesia at the moment is witnessing a remarkable increment. Even though the spiritual boom in the United States of America may be somewhat on the wane compared with the last decade, the statistics over the long run are sufficiently impressive.

At the declaration of independence, only five per cent were Christians. By the Civil War the figure had risen to twelve. At the turn of the century, one quarter of the people were included. Now the proportion is over sixty-two per cent. Nor is there any sign of any considerable let-up in the Church's missionary task. In spite of depleted personnel, the societies press on with the vital work. With the widespread use of modern means of communication —literature, radio, tapes, films, strips—the Church today is reaching more people with the message of life than ever before in its history. This is something in which to rejoice amidst much that would tend to depress.

When the Lord Jesus Christ was instructing His men about the course of future events, He told them; "This gospel of the kingdom will be preached throughout the whole world, as a testimony to all nations; and then the end will come" (Matt. 24:14). Mark also has "to all nations" (Mark 13:10). This universal dissemination of the faith had only just begun when Jerusalem was razed by the Romans. It continued throughout the Christian centuries and still does today. Right until the end, when Christ comes back, this task will be pursued. The good news will reach "the whole inhabited earth"—that is the meaning of the word (*oikoumenē* in Greek) translated "world"—the household or family of mankind. To discover how extensive and inclusive this is, we may turn to Acts 17:31, where Paul informs the Athenians that God "has fixed a day on which he will judge the world in righteousness by a man whom he has appointed." In Revelation 12:9, Satan is described as "the deceiver of the whole world," and again this same comprehensive term is used. The ecumenical movement today borrows it to indicate that the scope of Christian unity is world-wide. "All nations" is equally emphatic. It is echoed in the great commission: "Go therefore and make disciples of all nations, baptizing them in the name of the Father and of the Son and of the Holy Spirit, teaching them to observe all that I have commanded you; and lo, I am with you always, to the close of the age" (Matt. 28:19, 20). Our Lord's presence is promised throughout the period during which the gospel is to be preached—that is, right to the end.

The Christian message is called a gospel. It is good news. Originally the word *euanggelion* meant the reward given to a messenger when he delivered acceptable tidings, but then it came to be applied to the tidings themselves. This good news has to do with the kingdom—that is, the rule or supremacy of Christ. It is to be proclaimed as a testimony or witness. It is intended to arouse faith and to result in discipleship. This is the treasure which the Church has to share with the world. It can only prove faithful to its vocation as it offers the gospel in all its unadulterated fulness. That is more than ever necessary today. "It cannot be too emphatically stated," affirms Professor James S. Stewart, "that if contemporary evangelism is to make its full potential impact on the secularism of the age, it will have to go back more constantly and deliberately than it has done, and also more patiently and humbly, to its own fountain-head in the New Testament, and test there its message to this generation, re-examining in that light the content, the claim, and the communication of the message."

The entire missionary saga of the Christian Church, from the day of Pentecost to this very year in which we now live, is a fulfilment of our Lord's prophecy. Expansion is one of the signs of the times. The end will only come when the gospel has been taken to all nations. God's Word is to reach everywhere, so that all may be without excuse.

> Tell every man on earth,
>   The greatest and the least,
> Love called him from his birth
>   To be a king and priest.
>
> (Annie Matheson).

Official records show that ninety-six per cent of the people of the world now have the Bible, or some portion of it, in their own tongue. Another four per cent, and the task will be complete! It is said that the Coca-Cola Company of America has launched a five-year plan, to introduce everyone on earth to their product. Already there are but few countries where a "coke" has not penetrated. Soon they hope there will be none. And perhaps by then travellers will be indulging in it on the moon as well! If such ambitious plans are laid to circulate a fizzy drink, what ought the Church to be doing with the gospel in this day of unparalleled opportunity?

There lies the challenge of missions in our time. As we have seen, the number of Christians is increasing, but the population in most areas is doing so even more rapidly. Those who attended the World Congress on Evangelism in Berlin in 1966 will never be able to forget the inexorable ticking of the population clock in the entrance hall. Whilst discussions went on, we were reminded that every second, babies were being born around the world to add to the total number of those who are still to be won for Christ. There is no discharge in this war. The battle for souls will have to be fought right up to the moment when the Lord descends from heaven "with a cry of command, with the archangel's call, and with the sound of the trumpet of God" (1 Thess. 4:16). When the number of the elect has been made up "from every tribe and tongue and people and nation," then the end will come (Rev. 5:9).

A reporter from the *New York Journal* once called on Dr A. B. Simpson and asked him: "Do you know when the Lord is coming?" "Yes," Dr Simpson replied, "and I will tell you if you will promise to print just what I say, references and all." The reporter immediately whipped out his notebook. "Then put this down: 'This gospel of the kingdom shall be preached in all the world for a witness unto all nations; and then shall the end come' (Matt. 24:14 AV). Have you written the reference?" "Yes, what more?" "Nothing more." The reporter laid down his pencil and said, "Do you mean to say that you believe that when the gospel has been preached to all nations Jesus will return?" "Just that," agreed Dr Simpson. "Then," the reporter went on, "I think I begin to see daylight." "What do you think you see?" "Why, I see the motive and the motive-power of this movement."

How right he was! It is indeed this consideration which underlies all the Church's missionary endeavour. Because the task must be completed before the Lord returns, we are stimulated to press on with it more urgently. As Professor Oscar Cullman of Basle has observed: "The missionary work of the Church is the eschatological foretaste of the kingdom of God, and the biblical hope of the end constitutes the keenest incentive to action." "The gospel *must* first be preached to all nations" (Mark 13:10). There is a divine imperative involved. That is no doubt why Hudson Taylor could confess that the truth of the Lord's return had been the greatest spur to him in his missionary service.

When the Lord Jesus Christ was being tempted by the devil before He embarked on His ministry, He was taken to a very high mountain and shown all the kingdoms of the world and the glory of them. "All these I will give you, if you will fall down and worship me," promised Satan (Matt. 4:9). But our Lord refused to be seduced in that way. Already the Father had given Him the nations for His inheritance. He was not to win them by the exercise of military force or political influence. He would gain them by the gospel of His cross. And so, just before the close of His ministry, He was able to show His disciples a map of the world, as it were, and tell them that there was nowhere on it that would not one day be penetrated by the message of God's love. How astonishing that twelve men who had been introduced to the vision, should set about the task! Yet what the Lord predicted has actually come to pass. The gospel has now put a girdle round the earth. There is hardly a spot where it has not been heard. It may be that ours is the last generation to bear the torch. As we face the unfinished task, let us renew our solemn pledge to go and make Christ known.

Chapter Eighteen

REVIVAL

THERE is a widespread conviction amongst Christians that the only ultimate answer to our desperate world situation today lies in revival. "I see coming chaos as clearly as the shepherds saw the star of Bethlehem," writes Roger Babson. "Only one thing will stop this coming chaos—a sweeping spiritual awakening." "Speaking for our time," declares Stephen Olford, "I see no hope whatsoever, outside of the coming again of our Lord Jesus Christ or a mighty spiritual awakening." Billy Graham thinks that the alternatives are revival or revolution. Another writer has said: "Unless we are to see the war of wars usher in the night of nights, we need the revival of revivals."

What is the prospect for such a quickening in our time? We can only come to the conclusion that revival is always possible. The conditions of Pentecost may be recovered. Pentecost was not an isolated occasion: we must beware of reducing it to a museum piece. It did not happen just once, and shoot its bolt. There is a sense, of course, in which the events of the first Whitsuntide are unique and unrepeatable; there can never again be an original bestowment of the Spirit on the Church. But it would be quite wrong to conclude that therefore the experience of Pentecost cannot be renewed in succeeding generations. God is not exhausted. He did not run Himself down when He poured out His Spirit on all flesh. He is for ever capable of repeating the miracle. Indeed, that is what He rejoices to do. As D. L. Moody used to insist, Pentecost was but a specimen day: this is where the Church was meant to be.

As Dr Stanley Jones wrote in *The Christ of Every Road*: "The Church is not living in Pentecost. It is living between Easter and Pentecost. Easter stands for a life wrought out and offered. Pentecost stands for life appropriated and lived to its full. The Church stands hesitant between the two, hesitant, hence comparatively impotent. If the Church would move up to Pentecost, nothing could stop it—NOTHING." The capitals are his, and how challenging they are! This is what is required more than anything else today. Revival is the answer.

A bishop who was deeply concerned about the need for spiritual improvement in one of the parishes of his diocese, wrote to the incumbent and said: "Dear Vicar, I propose to come to your parish to conduct a quiet day." But the vicar, knowing all too well the condition of his people, wrote in return: "My dear Bishop, It is not a quiet day that we need in this parish—we need an earthquake." That is the plight of the modern Church. Only a Pentecostal earthquake will shake it into life again.

This is just what revival does; it brings life, and it brings it *again*. That is its very nature. The word "revival" implies a previous bestowal of life. Only that which has once been alive can be revived. The world cannot be revived. Men who are dead in trespasses and sins cannot be revived. Thank God they can be given spiritual life in Christ, but only those who have known such a new birth can properly be revived. That is why the Bible insists that revival has to do with the people of God. "Wilt thou not revive us again, that thy people may rejoice in thee?" enquires the Psalmist (Ps. 85:6). Revival restores the Church to the level of Pentecost. It transplants it once more into the context of Acts two.

Revival appears to be a recurring sign of the times: ever and again throughout the Christian centuries, God has graciously renewed His people. "It looks as though there were seasons in the course of history," wrote the distinguished Quaker, Dr Rufus M. Jones, "which are like vernal equinoxes of the Spirit, when fresh initiations into more life occur, when new installations of life seem to break in and enlarge the empire of man's divine estate." There is a certain rhythm of revival running through the years. Historians have plotted its course. Such a season of refreshing from the Lord's hand was observable in the primitive Church. It was granted again in a movement of the Spirit under Montanus, which, although condemned as heretical, nevertheless won over so notable a figure as Tertullian. Even in the darkness of Roman dominance—what Luther called the Babylonian Captivity of the Church—God did not leave Himself altogether without witness. There were reformers before the Reformation who were instruments of awakening—Hus, Wyclif, Tauler and the like. The Protestant Reformation itself represents the most significant revival since Pentecost, and its benefits have endured to our day. There was a revival in Britain during the Puritan commonwealth—the most spiritual era in our history—and even afterwards, when in the Great Plague of London many of the established clergy fled for their lives, and the ejected ministers fearlessly returned to their former charges to lead a notable work of God. The Evangelical revival of the eighteenth century under Whitefield and the Wesleys, and the '59 revival of the nineteenth century represent further evidences of this recurring sign of the times. These outbursts of blessing cannot be confined within any prescribed limits, nor can they be predicted. They have their origin in the sovereign, inscrutable will of God. The wind of the Spirit blows where it lists. As Dr Alexander Whyte used to say, "there is a divine mystery about revivals."

In a priceless little book, long out of print, Griffith John confronted the issue which is uppermost in so many Christian minds today. "Is a new Pentecost possible to us?" he enquired. "To this question there can be but one answer. It must be possible. We are still in the dispensation of the Spirit. The might of God was not exhausted on that day. That baptism was only an earnest and a pledge of a still further and fuller manifestation of God to man." We have seen how Moody regarded Pentecost as a specimen day. George Bowen of Bombay added another and significant phrase: "the specimen day to accompany the promise." God has undertaken to visit His people with revival, and in case we should be tempted to doubt the likelihood, we have only to look at Pentecost.

Revival, then, is a sign of the intervening times between the Lord's departure and His return. It was when He ascended that the Spirit was poured out. The Spirit is still being poured out, and will be until the end of the age. That is the inference of the future continuous tense in Acts 2:17 (citing Joel 2:28)—"I will go on pouring out my Spirit upon all flesh." The prophet Joel telescopes the entire period from the giving of the Spirit to the return of our Lord in a single vision. The first part of it was fulfilled at Pentecost—that which is recorded in verses 17 and 18 of Acts two. But what follows in verses 19 and 20 quite obviously is not yet fulfilled—"And I will show wonders in the heaven above and signs on the earth beneath, blood, and fire, and vapour of smoke; the sun shall be turned into darkness and the moon into blood, before the day of the Lord comes, the great and manifest day." This has to do with the end. The supernatural phenomena described so vividly here will be displayed only in conjunction with the second advent, as Jesus Himself forecast (Matt. 24:29). In Joel's prophecy, the stretch of time between Pentecost and the Parousia is viewed synoptically as from the divine perspective.

It is held by some scholars that this implies that as there was a revival in connection with the coming of the Spirit at the beginning of the Church's history, so there will be a revival in connection with the coming of Christ at its end. In an important chapter of his book *In the Day of Thy Power*, Arthur Wallis has expounded the salient Old Testament passages which relate to the latter rain of promise and its bearing on revival. It is to these that an appeal is made by those who expect an unusual awakening before the close of the age. In Palestine, there is a prolonged dry season which runs from April to October. This is broken by what the Scripture calls the former rain. The farmer is dependent on it for softening the iron-hard soil and making it suitable for ploughing and sowing. These heavy falls are followed by many weeks of intermittent showers. Then, as harvest time draws near, the latter rain of ingathering helps to swell the grain prior to the season of reaping. "Let us fear the Lord our God, who gives the rain in the season" says Jeremiah (5:24), "the autumn (former) rain and the spring (latter) rain, and keeps for us the weeks appointed for the harvest."

Now according to this interpretation, Pentecost is the spiritual fulfilment of the former rain. Within the mainstream of the Church age, we can look for scattered showers such as continued at intervals throughout the Jewish winter, for we are told that at no period do they cease altogether. This corresponds to that element of revival which is a continuing sign of the times. But before the return of Christ we may expect, as Wallis claims, "a season of mighty outpourings, eclipsing all that the Church has experienced since the Reformation, and only comparable in character and in power with the former rain of the early Church." If this theory is correct, then it means that at the end of the gospel era there will be a revival as powerful as Pentecost itself and much more widespread. It will be a time when God's people seek Him, and He comes and rains salvation on them (Hosea 10:12).

Throughout these studies we have deliberately refrained from speculation beyond the disclosures of the Word. We dare not pretend to a knowledge of dates and seasons which the Father has fixed by His own authority (Acts 1:7). Even the Lord Jesus Christ Himself whilst in the flesh was unaware of the divine timetable so far as the last things are concerned. Much less should we presume to dogmatize. But if there is to be a great expansion before the end, it may well be that revival will accompany it. Should this happen in our day, how our hearts would be warmed to see it! "Ask rain from the Lord in the season of the spring rain," is the injunction of Zechariah (10:1). Let a cry for revival go up from the world-wide Church. That is how the bride would best be prepared to meet the Bridegroom when He comes.